Faithful God

An exposition of the book of Ruth

by

Sinclair B. Ferguson

First published 2005
Reprinted 2007, 2009
This edition 2013

ISBN 978-1-85049 247 4

Evangelical Movement of Wales

The EMW works in both Welsh and English and seeks to help Christians and churches by running children's camps and family conferences, providing theological training and events for ministers, running Christian bookshops and a conference centre, publishing magazines and books.

Bryntirion Press is a ministry of EMW

Published by Bryntirion Press, Bryntirion, Bridgend CF31 4DX, Wales, in association Evangelical Press, Faverdale North, Darlington, DL3 0PH, UK.

For John and Ruth Murdoch

'The LORD your God is God, the faithful God,
who keeps covenant and steadfast love'
(Deuteronomy 7:9)

'Faithful God,
Faithful God,
All-sufficient one,
I worship you.
Shalom, my peace,
My strong deliverer,
I lift you up,
Faithful God.'

Chris Bowater[1]

'You have been my help,
and in the shadow of your wings I will sing for joy.'
(Psalm 63:7)

Contents

Preface

This study of the Book of Ruth has its origins in a series of addresses given at the English-speaking conference of the Evangelical Movement of Wales in Aberystwyth in August 1996.

The spoken word and the written word are very different kinds of communication. Thus when a transcription of the addresses with a request for publication was sent to me I was not optimistic that the material would ever see the light of day. Turning spoken exposition into a written form, at least in my experience, takes longer than simply writing from scratch! That has been true of this little book also. No one is more surprised than I that, almost a decade later, these studies are now appearing in print. But preparing the material for publication has given me great pleasure in working again through the Book of Ruth.

The Aberystwyth Conference is a special event. To speak in the happy atmosphere of the packed Great Hall of the University of Wales, to enjoy the hearty singing of hundreds of Welsh voices, and morning by morning to trace with so many eager Christians the—at times nerve-racking, at times romantic—plot line of the Book of Ruth, was for me a memorable experience.

There can—and should be—great pleasure in the corporate study of Scripture. Sometimes people say as they leave church, 'I enjoyed that . . . Oh! I shouldn't say "enjoy", should I? . . . but you know what I mean, don't you?' I have learned to respond: 'Of course you should say it! We were made to "enjoy God" and his Word!' A parenthesis in the original transcript of these expositions has reminded me of the shared enjoyment of the Aberystwyth Conference: 'Much laughter on the tape at this point!' Readers will search these pages in vain for the cause of that particular merriment, but I nevertheless hope that the pleasures of God and his Word will still be sensed through the printed page.

Several debts have been incurred in connection with this book. In particular I would like to thank David Kingdon (now retired from the editorial management of the Press) for his encouragement to publish this material, and also the present staff of the Press. I hope that the publication of these pages will in a small way recompense them all for their patience.

The immediate stimulus to work on this book was the rediscovery of a computer disk marked 'Ruth—Aberystwyth 1996'. In the words of the book of Ruth this 'so happened' a few weeks before the marriage of our daughter. Her name is Ruth.

Sinclair B Ferguson
Westminster Theological Seminary
Dallas
Texas

Chapter One
Ruth: her story and ours

'He who dwells in the shelter of the Most High will abide in the shadow of the Almighty. I will say to the LORD, "My refuge and my fortress, my God, in whom I trust." For he will deliver you from the snare of the fowler and from the deadly pestilence. He will cover you with his pinions, and under his wings you will find refuge; his faithfulness is a shield and buckler.' (Psalm 91:1-4)

The book of Ruth is not a work of deep theological reasoning like Paul's epistle to the Romans, yet it is full of theology. It is not a magnificent symphony on the work of Christ like the Gospel of John, yet it ultimately points to the coming of Christ. It is not full of vivid apocalyptic imagery like the book of the Revelation, yet it traces the details of God's working in the unfolding of the events of history. It is not basic instruction about the kingdom of God like the Sermon on the Mount, yet it contains important lessons about life in that kingdom.

The book of Ruth does all this by teaching the timeless lessons illustrated in the lives of its three main characters, Naomi, Ruth and Boaz. Its historical narrative carries a message of lasting contemporary relevance. As with every other part of the Bible, there are important reasons to study this book.

God-breathed Scripture

When we study Scripture we ought to have in mind Paul's words:

All Scripture is breathed out by God and profitable for teaching, for reproof, for correction, and for training in righteousness, that the man of God may be competent, equipped for every good work. (2 *Timothy* 3:16-17)

In our English Bibles there is a chapter division at the end of these words. But it is somewhat misleading, for Paul goes on to urge Timothy to preach the word in such a way that it will accomplish the very goals for which he has just said it was originally given. He is to 'preach the word; be ready in season and out of season; reprove, rebuke, and exhort, with complete patience and teaching' (2 Timothy 4:2).

Thus, whenever we turn to Scripture, whether to a passage, section or book, we should ask ourselves:

1. What does it teach us?
2. In what areas of our lives does it rebuke us?
3. What healing, restoring, transforming effect does this teaching have?
4. How does this section of Scripture equip me to serve Christ better?

When we read, or listen to, the exposition of Scripture (Paul is here urging Timothy to preach it, and how to do so), the result, whether directly or indirectly, should be increased understanding in each of these four areas.

So, in studying the book of Ruth, we want to look out for:

1. *Doctrine*. Teaching about God and his ways with us that will illumine our minds and our understanding of the gospel.
2. *Reproof*. Areas in which the Spirit will touch our consciences and convict us of sin and failure.
3. *Correction.* This word sometimes carries a negative

connotation for us, but the term Paul uses (*epanorthōsis*) expresses the ideas of restoration and healing. It appears outside of the New Testament in a medical context for mending and restoring a broken limb. In the Septuagint[1] (which Paul knew) it was used, for example, of the 'rebuilding' of the broken wall of Jerusalem.

4. *Equipping.* As a result of studying, understanding and making the Scriptures our own, we should be the better prepared to serve our Lord Jesus Christ.

Redemptive history

The book of Ruth is part of the biblical narrative of redemptive history. It describes one more stage in the purposes of God as they moved inexorably towards the final redemption of his people through Jesus Christ.

No detail of the lives of our loved ones is insignificant to those of us who love them. That is also true of Jesus. When we come by faith to love him, the details of his life, the story of his background, his family history, all come to have a new fascination for us.

This is where the book of Ruth comes in. It focuses like a microscope on part of the detailed preparation God made in order to fulfil his purposes in redemptive history. Apparently the story of a small and insignificant family, it is actually one of the building blocks in God's preparatory work as he sovereignly directed history towards the coming of the Saviour Jesus Christ. In fact, the message of the book of Ruth cannot be fully understood apart from the coming of our Lord Jesus Christ. In that sense, studying it will help us to understand Christ himself—and, indeed, the whole Bible—more fully and clearly.

Divine providence

The book of Ruth shows us in miniature form, but in considerable detail, how wise God's sovereign purposes really are.

We are not able to detect with perfect clarity the hand of God in the circumstances of our lives, far less see where he is heading with them. But when we find his autograph in the narratives of biblical history, we begin to recognise the same or similar patterns and principles emerging in our own lives too—and so we learn to see his handwriting in our own experiences.

The English poet William Cowper, who struggled a great deal to come to terms with his melancholic disposition and frequent deep depression, teaches us about this principle in his famous words:

God moves in a mysterious way
His wonders to perform.
He plants his footsteps in the sea
And rides upon the storm.[2]

The problem with looking for footsteps planted in the sea (Cowper was probably thinking about Psalm 77:19) is that they immediately become invisible. God moves in mysterious ways; we do not have immediate access to his blueprints; we cannot second guess his purposes. We must learn to trust and obey him on the basis of his word of promise to us. One of the reasons we can do so is because of the evidence given to us in the Scriptures of his wise providence.

Finite creatures can never fully comprehend what an infinite God is doing. Those who are always sure of the details of God's plans for them need to be treated with some suspicion—they may be in for a shock! But here in the book of Ruth, God allows us to see the kind of thing he does, so that we may trust him when we see similar patterns being woven into our own lives.

At the time, of course, what God was accomplishing in the lives of Naomi, Ruth and Boaz was far from clear to any of them—even though these were the three people most involved in the story! More than that, right at the end of the story, the author shows how God was doing far more than they could have realised during their lifetimes.

In fact, as Christians in the New Testament era, we know even more than the author of the book of Ruth about what God was planning and working out through the lives of its central characters. In this way, God is saying to us, 'Do you see how I planted my footsteps in the sea in the lives of these my children in past days? Let me show you how I did that. This is the kind of God I am; that is the kind of thing I do; and that is precisely what you may expect me to do in your lives, too. Trust me! I know exactly what I am doing.' As we learn from God's Word in this way, it becomes profitable to us.

What we see in the narrative sections of the Bible, then, is the way in which God takes up ordinary people into his purposes and uses them in ways inexplicable in terms of the ordinary. In these passages and books God shows us how he sovereignly works out his perfect will.

Reflections

So, as we read the book of Ruth, we discover it is a kind of mirror in which we see four different reflections.

- The first is that of the various characters who appear on the stage of the narrative: Naomi, Ruth and Boaz, along with some others who play secondary roles in the drama.

- The second is the reflection of God himself. All historical narratives in the Old Testament are written from a specific point of view, sometimes referred to as the perspective of 'the omniscient narrator'. The voice that tells the story always knows more than the characters involved in it. The narrator has access to God's thoughts and plans. He speaks from hindsight. His voice gives us hints and clues about what God is doing in the situation. If we listen carefully to it, we will begin to detect the hand of God.
- The third reflection is, of course, that of Jesus. In one way or another all Scripture points to him and leads to him (Luke 24:27; 2 Timothy 3:15). It does so in many different ways. So when we read the Bible, we should ask the question: 'How does this book or passage point ultimately to Christ?' As we read Ruth, we will see Christ's reflection appearing at different points in different ways.
- The fourth reflection is that of our own lives. We will notice this at different levels. Sometimes we will learn what to do and what to avoid. But, more fundamentally, we will see that when God works in our lives today, he continues to use the patterns of grace that are worked out in Scripture. In this way we begin to learn how God shapes our lives in order to make them like Christ (cf. Romans 6:17; 8:29). As we watch what God does in the lives of others, the manner of his working in our own lives becomes clearer.

The book of Ruth records experiences of joy and sorrow. It tells a story of home life, romance and marriage, of unexpected conversion and radical consecration. The book of Ruth is *multum in parvo* (much in little)—a little book containing far more about God than its size would suggest. Here we will find many lessons about his grace and his providence.

Ruth 1: 1-22

IN the days when the judges ruled there was a famine in the land, and a man of Bethlehem in Judah went to sojourn in the country of Moab, he and his wife and his two sons. 2The name of the man was Elimelech and the name of his wife Naomi, and the names of his two sons were Mahlon and Chilion. They were Ephrathites from Bethlehem in Judah. They went into the country of Moab and remained there. 3But Elimelech, the husband of Naomi, died, and she was left with her two sons. 4These took Moabite wives; the name of one was Orpah and the name of the other Ruth. They lived there about ten years, 5and both Mahlon and Chilion died, so that the woman was left without her two sons and her husband.

6Then she arose with her daughters-in-law to return from the country of Moab, for she had heard in the fields of Moab that the LORD had visited his people and given them food. 7So she set out from the place where she was with her two daughters-in-law, and they went on the way to return to the land of Judah. 8But Naomi said to her two daughters-in-law, 'Go, return each of you to her mother's house. May the LORD deal kindly with you, as you have dealt with the dead and with me. 9The LORD grant that you may find rest, each of you in the house of her husband!' Then she kissed them, and they lifted up their voices and wept. 10And they said to her, 'No, we will return with you to your people.' 11But Naomi said, 'Turn back, my daughters; why will you go with me? Have I yet sons in my womb that they may become your husbands? 12Turn back, my daughters; go your way, for I am too old to have a husband. If I should say I have hope, even if I should have a husband this night and should bear sons, 13would you therefore wait till they were grown? Would you 19 therefore refrain from marrying? No, my daughters, for it is exceedingly bitter to me for your sake that the hand of the LORD has gone out against me.' 14Then they lifted up their voices and wept again. And Orpah kissed her mother-in-law, but Ruth clung to her.

15And she said, 'See, your sister-in-law has gone back to her people and to her gods; return after your sister-in-law.' 16But Ruth said, 'Do not urge me to leave you or to return from following you. For where you go I will go, and where you lodge I will lodge. Your people shall be my people, and your God my God. 17Where you die I will die, and there will I be buried. May the LORD do so to me and more also if anything but death parts me from you.' 18And when Naomi saw that she was determined to go with her, she said no more.

19So the two of them went on until they came to Bethlehem. And when they came to Bethlehem, the whole town was stirred because of them. And the women said, 'Is this Naomi?' 20She said to them, 'Do not call me Naomi; call me Mara, for the Almighty has dealt very bitterly with me. 21I went away full, and the LORD has brought me back empty. Why call me Naomi, when the Lord has testified against me and the Almighty has brought calamity upon me?'

22So Naomi returned, and Ruth the Moabite her daughter-in-law with her, who returned from the country of Moab. And they came to Bethlehem at the beginning of barley harvest.

Chapter Two
Narrative of a surprising conversion

'And when . . . you . . . return to the LORD your God, you and your children, and obey his voice in all that I command you today, with all your heart and with all your soul, then the LORD your God will restore your fortunes and have compassion on you, and he will gather you again from all the peoples where the LORD your God has scattered you . . . And the LORD your God will bring you into the land that your fathers possessed, that you may possess it. And he will make you more prosperous and numerous than your fathers.' (Deuteronomy 30:1-3,5)

'All Gaul', wrote Julius Caesar, 'is divided into three parts'.[3] So, basically, is all great narrative. It is composed of a problem, an unravelling of it, and a solution to it.

The first chapter of Ruth both introduces us to this pattern and illustrates it in embryo. It describes three parts of a spiritual journey. Each of these segments brings us to a different geographical location. These are like stations on the rail track of God's grace. He means us to pause at each of them to learn something new about how he works in the affairs of his children.

A tale of three scenes

The first scene (1:1-5) describes the journey of a family who emigrate east from Bethlehem to the land of Moab, and it is largely set in that pagan country.

The second scene, in the central part of the chapter (1:6-18), takes place a decade or so later. It describes a return journey from Moab. The action (like two-thirds of this book, it is mainly dialogue) is located at a crossroads between Moab and Bethlehem. Here we are invited to pause and reflect on the way in which God is moving his sovereign purposes forwards.

The chapter (indeed, the rest of the book) ends back in Bethlehem (1:19-22). It is not insignificant that all this takes place when 'there was no king in Israel' (Judges 21:25), yet in the very town where Israel's greatest king would later be reared (1 Samuel 16:1) and where the King of kings would be born (cf. Micah 5:2; Matthew 2:1).

Turning point

Central to the whole chapter are the most famous words in the book—Ruth's memorable statement to her mother-in- law:

> *Do not urge me to leave you or to return from following you. For where you go I will go, and where you lodge I will lodge. Your people shall be my people, and your God my God. Where you die I will die, and there will I be buried. May the LORD do so to me and more also if anything but death parts me from you. (Ruth 1:16-17)*

One of the characteristics of Old Testament narrative— indeed, of any good story—is that it has a centre point, which is often the turning point. That is why, in Hebrew narratives, the most important thing often lies at the centre of a passage or even of a single verse.[4] We see this in many of the psalms. At the beginning of the psalm the writer is going down—into difficulties, doubts, even despair. But then the psalm ends with his spirits lifted up and his heart encouraged. The key to interpreting the change is to notice what lies at the centre of the psalm, where the turning point comes, and to observe what causes it.

The same is true of this story. It begins and ends in Bethlehem (vv.1,22). But its centre point lies in what takes place between Moab and Bethlehem. This is a turning point, geographically and also spiritually. We might even say it is the conversion point.

Ruth's words, as we shall see, are more than an expression of human devotion: 'Where you go I will go; I will die where you die; let nothing but death separate you from me.' In fact, even here it is the central statement that is the key to the whole thing: 'Your people shall be my people, and your God my God.' These words do reveal deep human affection, devotion and dogged determination. But they are much more than that: they constitute a confession of personal conversion. 'Your God will be my God' is not so much a statement of undying love for a mother-in-law (amazing though that may be!), as a profession of faith.

What has taken place at the turning point in this whole chapter, at the crossroads between Moab and Bethlehem, is a deeper turning point: the spiritual conversion of Ruth! Indeed, if we were Hebrews listening to this story for the first time in our own language, we would probably have picked up signals that this was what was happening. That is why the ancient Jewish rabbis thought of Ruth as a proselyte convert (and sometimes tried to squeeze out of her words a commitment to the basic boundary markers of Judaism, such as the Sabbath).[5]

Words that give signals

These signals are not always as clear in our English translations as they would have been to the first readers of Ruth.

Many modern Bible translations are made on the principle of what is called 'dynamic equivalence'. Here, the translator asks not simply, 'What are the English equivalents of these Hebrew or Greek words?' but in addition the further question, 'How would we actually say this in English?'

Other—usually older—translations (although *The English Standard Version* is a modern exception) try as far as is reasonable to draw us into the original languages with their original metaphors and word pictures. Some of these English translations have also tried to help us read the text with a sense of its original Hebrew and Greek by translating the same Hebrew or Greek word by the same English word every time it appears—if possible.

This can make for a very wooden translation, but it does have the advantage of highlighting something very important in Old Testament storytelling—something the Hebrews greatly enjoyed—the repetition of a phrase or word as a clue to the plot and meaning of the story. Sometimes a word with several possible meanings, or a word that meant something special in the broader context of God's Word, could function as a way of saying: Do you get the message? Do you see what is really happening, what God is doing here?

There is an example of this in Ruth chapter 1 in the repeated use of the Hebrew word shub.

The meaning of *shub*

In Ruth chapter 1, the Hebrew verb *shub* is used over and over again. It is translated by: 'return' (vv.6,7,8,10,16,22); 'turn back' (vv.11,12); 'gone back'(v.15); 'brought back' (v.21). This slight variation in translation is excellent from one point of view. Repetition does not often make for enjoyable English. It dulls the style with a sense of sameness. But the variation in translation here, legitimate as it is, obscures a significant element in the way in which the story is told in the Hebrew Bible. The constant repetition of this particular verb is significant because it is not only the Hebrew word for 'return', but it is the Old Testament's main word for turning back to God's covenant grace and mercy—for repentance, for conversion.

By using this theologically important term, the author of Ruth is giving us a hint: 'Don't you see what is happening here, underneath the surface? Do you see what God is doing here? This is a conversion.' Indeed, to borrow words from the title of Jonathan Edwards' famous account of the revival in eighteenth-century New England, this is *A Narrative of a Surprising Conversion.*

The verb *shub* runs like a melody line through the whole story. When we hear it again and again, we cannot possibly miss what this story is about. *It is about turning back to God.* It is about returning to his grace. Indeed, this is one of the greatest—and perhaps the most detailed—account in the Old Testament of how God sovereignly works to bring someone to faith.

Chapter 1 is a tale of three scenes.

Emigration

Scene one takes us from Bethlehem to Moab. It tells a story of the need and suffering of a small family, of wrong steps taken to deal with their difficulties, and of disastrous consequences. Yet it also underlines that the saving purposes of God ordinarily begin in his hidden, and sometimes dark, providences. Frequently God's hand is placed on the sufferings and trials of an individual in order for his grip to take hold of someone else.

The opening words set the scene for us. First of all, they provide us with a chronology. The events of the book of Ruth take place 'In the days when the judges ruled', somewhere in the two-hundred-year period between 1250 BC and 1050 BC. But then the author adds words that set the scene spiritually: 'there was a famine in the land'.

How can a famine have spiritual significance? God had promised to give his people a land flowing with milk and honey where he would bless them (Exodus 3:8). No area was more highly favoured than the land around Bethlehem (the name literally means 'House of Bread'). But 'in the days when the judges ruled', there was a famine even there. In fact, the statement 'the days when the judges ruled' is not simply a chronological or historical marker but a theological one. Remember the closing verse of the book of Judges? 'In those days there was no king in Israel. Everyone did what was right in his own eyes' (Judges 21:25). It is a refrain repeated from Judges 17:6: 'In those days there was no king in Israel. Everyone did what was right in his own eyes.'

What was happening in the days of the judges—the days between Israel's settlement in Canaan and the appointment of Saul as the first king? What is the significance of the fact that 'there was a famine in the land'?

Famine

When God had made his covenant with his people, Moses had explained in detail its implications for them. Wonderful blessings would come to God's people if they were faithful to his covenant promises: terrible judgements and curses would result from any unfaithfulness or apostasy (Deuteronomy 27; 28). The curses included what God would do to the land and to the food supply—this land that had once been flowing with milk and honey (Exodus 3:8).

He had once cursed the ground in the Garden of Eden because of his son Adam's sin (Genesis 3:17-18), and he had sent his flood in judgement on the whole earth (Genesis 6–9). Now he said that if his adopted son Israel disobeyed him, he would make the heavens like brass, the crops would fail and the harvest would be blighted (Deuteronomy 28:15ff.).

Now, 'in the days when the judges ruled'—actually, days when the people were unruly—this was really happening! God's word was coming true. There was famine; the fields were bare; the barns were empty. And the author of Ruth understands that this is not an accident of history but the outworking of God's covenant promise: 'Turn away from me and I will send physical deprivation to make you face up to your sin and your hardness of heart. Trust and obey me again and I will bless you and your harvests will be bountiful.' God had, as it were, switched on the amber warning light. It was a clear signal that his people were drifting from him and needed to repent.

That was the picture throughout the whole nation. But national scenes are composed of multitudes of smaller family scenes like the one described in Ruth 1. Thus we are introduced to Elimelech, his wife Naomi, and their two sons Mahlon and Chilion (which seem to mean something like 'Weakling' and 'Pining'). God is saying to this family, as well as to the whole nation: 'Little family set in my covenant community in these needy days, return to me. Call upon me and I will have mercy on you. Repent of your sins. I will come to you with forgiveness and grace. I will restore to you everything that has now been taken from you. I do not desire to do you harm, but to do you good. Surely you know that? Then return to me.' He had promised that if they would:

> *return to the LORD your God . . . then the LORD your God will restore your fortunes and have compassion on you . . . will make you abundantly prosperous in all the work of your hand, in the fruit of your womb . . . and in the fruit of your ground. (Deuteronomy 30:2,3,9)*

Illegal immigrants?

But instead of *turning back* to the Lord, this little family *turn their backs on* the Lord, and go to live in Moab (v.1, the verb is *shub*).

In the light of the rest of Scripture, an ominous atmosphere surrounds their choice of destination. The king of Moab, Balak, had once hired Balaam to curse Israel (Numbers 22:1ff.). The name Moab was associated with pagan religion and worship. Earlier in the period of the judges, in the chastening providence of God, Eglon, the infamously fat king of Moab, had defeated Israel and made her a vassal people for eighteen years until the left-handed Ehud the Benjaminite was raised up by God to deliver them (Judges 3:14-30).

True, emigration in times of famine or religious persecution has a long and honourable history. It is not only an understandable but sometimes a courageous and costly move. Think of the little bands of pilgrims who in the seventeenth century sailed three thousand miles across the powerful Atlantic Ocean in boats little bigger than a house, in the hope of finding freedom to worship and provide for their families. But, for Naomi and her family, emigration involves turning their backs upon the Lord's word and his summons to repentance. Thus, instead of seeking grace, Elimelech's little family—did he make the decision himself, or in consultation with Naomi? or did she perhaps even drive him to it?—decide that if God will not provide what they need for their lives, they will take it for themselves. And so they go to live 'for a while' (v.1, NIV), so they think, as alien residents in Moab.

Why is this so serious?

For one thing, they are forsaking the only place on earth God has specifically given to his people, the place in which he has promised to bless them and provide for all their needs. In the old covenant there were particular geographical spaces and times that God had designated as 'holy'. These were specific places where God promised to meet with his people. Eventually they formed a series of concentric circles: the Promised Land, the city of Jerusalem, the Temple and, at the centre, the Holy of Holies. The Promised Land was the one place on earth where, whatever happened, you could be safe sheltering under the shadow of the Almighty (Psalm 91:1ff.).

But the word of God does not please this family. Theyseek to take the provision God promises apart from the repentance God requires. They go to live among the Moabites—a people whose roots lay in the sad story recorded in Genesis 19. Moab himself was the son of the incestuous relationship between Lot and his older daughter.

Do Elimelech and Naomi intend only a brief sojourn? Ten years later Naomi is still there (v.4). When we turn our backs on the Lord's word we never intend to do it for long. It is only going to be for a little while, over a small matter. But it rarely works out that way.

Nightmare

During those ten years Naomi finds herself in a personal nightmare. First of all, her husband Elimelech dies. Then the two boys—predictably—marry Moabite women.

The Old Testament teaches us that the children of a mixed marriage between a covenant child and a Moabite person were not allowed into the assembly of the Lord for ten generations, that is, for 400 years—by that time only the most avid searcher of family trees would know where these people came from (Deuteronomy 23:3-6).[6] If that seems harsh, we should remember that everything about Moab spelled alienation from God and from his promises. Its worship involved the 'gods' of nature. Such a fertility cult, which in the Ancient Near East often included sexual activity and ritual prostitution, was an abomination to the Lord.

But worse is to come. As though Naomi's grief were not enough, after they have lived in Moab for a decade, both Mahlon and Chilion die. Picture Naomi standing at her third grave. See her sad and tortured face. Are there tears, or is she now so emotionally exhausted by sorrow that she is unable to find relief in tears—a mourner who cannot weep? Naomi is left without her two sons and her husband (v.5). She is—and this is something to which the Old Testament is particularly sensitive—left in the position of someone experiencing one of the most painful curses: there is no living fruit from her womb. She is bereft, alienated, and lonely.

In these cruel losses, she must feel that God has thrust his sword into her heart, twisted it, and then thrust it in deeper. It is surely tragedy enough to lose a husband. But why has the sovereign Lord thrust the sword in again and then twisted it round in her soul? 'Weakling' and 'Pining' might be the meaning of her sons' names; but the early sense of their physical frailty suggested by these names was no preparation for the stunning and numbing pain Naomi now experiences in their premature deaths.

It is hardly surprising, then, to read Naomi's words in verses 13 and 20-21:

> *It is exceedingly bitter for me for your sake that the hand of the LORD has gone out against me . . . Do not call me Naomi ['Pleasantness']; call me Mara ['Bitter'], for the Almighty has dealt very bitterly with me. I went away full, and the LORD has brought me back empty.*

Most of us would not dare to say: 'The explanation for your experience is this: *the Lord has afflicted you.*' That would seem to be insensitive in the extreme. We would be more likely to put our hands to our mouths and say as little as possible. Words would sound like platitudes if they came from the lips of those who know little about such inner pain and loss. But here Naomi herself says, 'The Almighty has dealt very bitterly with me.'

Although it is impossible to be dogmatic about it, Naomi's words do not seem to mean, 'I am very bitter', or, 'The Lord has embittered me', but that her pathway has been a bitter one. For there is evidence here and at the end of the chapter that she wants to be called Mara rather than Naomi, not because the Lord has made her a twisted, bitter woman, but because bitter experiences have been the hallmark of her life. Out of these bitter experiences God will do something sweet and new. But in the event, life has become very bleak. Indeed, she must have cried out in her dark hours, 'God, what have I done to deserve this?'

Would you dare to say to her, 'The explanation is simple: you left the Promised Land; you deserved everything you got'? Is that an adequate explanation? Probably others had done the same thing without suffering such horrendous consequences. Why is Naomi experiencing such a catalogue of grief? Yes, Naomi and her husband did sin, no matter who took the lead. But the significance of her experience is far more complex than simply being a punishment for sin. True, we really deserve nothing from God's hand but punishment. But we cannot draw over-simple equations between the suffering of this woman and the sin in which her family engaged. Naomi's suffering is not explicable merely in terms of her sin. If it were that simple, she might be able to cope with it. But God is too majestic, too infinitely wise in his providences, to be reduced to simple formulae when he brings his children into experiences of suffering. There must surely be a deeper analysis of these events.

Scene two takes place at the end of the decade in the 'far country'.

Decision time

In Naomi's circumstances, many people would turn their backs on God and shake clenched fists in his face, saying, 'How can you be a God of love and grace when this is happening to me?' Naomi does not do that.

A sharp knife can be a destructive weapon in the hands of a murderer, but it can also be an instrument of healing in the hands of a surgeon. Everything depends on the hands that use it. In this case, God is working like a skilled surgeon. The painful surgery is part of a healing process. Thus, chastened by sore providence, Naomi seems to have been prepared by God to respond positively to the news she hears in Moab—perhaps from some passing merchant. The Lord has come to help his people by providing food for them (1:6). Covenant blessings have returned; there is a supply of food again for the needy. The Lord opens Naomi's heart, and graciously brings her back through bitter experiences to his blessing.

Naomi returns (the verb is *shub* again); she repents.

Repentance

Naomi's return gives us some insight into what motivates genuine repentance towards God, what the New Testament calls 'repentance that leads to life' (Acts 11:18). Her (and our) need for repentance is, of course, rooted in the fact of sin and the subsequent judgement and condemnation of God's holy law. But knowing we are condemned does not—on its own—lead us to repentance. That requires God's covenant mercy—the good news that there is food in Bethlehem. The Hebrew of Ruth 1:6 ('given them food') is literally 'given them bread' (*lechem*, from which Bethlehem— *beth:* 'house', and *lechem*: 'bread/food'—comes).

Neither Naomi, nor the author of Ruth, nor those who first heard the story, will have made the final connection we are able to make in the light of the New Testament. The prodigal son is encouraged to return to his father's house because there is 'more than enough bread' (Luke 15:17). More than that, it is ultimately because God has shown his grace in giving Jesus, the Bread of Life, born in Bethlehem, that we know he will pardon the repentant, and are therefore encouraged to turn back to him. As the *Westminster Confession of Faith* well says, it is a sense of the mercy of God that brings us to repentance:

> *Repentance unto life is an evangelical grace . . . by it, a sinner, out of the sight and sense not only of the danger, but also of the filthiness and odiousness of his sins, as contrary to the holy nature, and righteous law of God; and upon the apprehension of His mercy in Christ to such as are penitent, so grieves for . . . his sins, as to turn from them all unto God . . .*[7]

So we can sing:

> *Thou know'st the way to bring me back,*
> *My fallen spirit to restore.*[8]

But what a way!

A number of years ago, a friend whom God had wonderfully prospered developed the deeply distressing symptoms of a rare and fatal disease. I still often reflect on his telling me how God had earlier brought him through affliction and trial. He said, 'I have learned what the psalmist meant when he said, "Before I was afflicted I went astray, but now I keep your word"' (Psalm 119:67). That is what we are meant to learn from the scenes in Moab. The Lord has come to the aid of his people. Naomi plans to return to Bethlehem. Her daughters-in-law express a desire to go with her. They leave the place where they have been living and set out on the road that will take them back to the land of Judah.

At some point on this journey Naomi stops and addresses Orpah and Ruth. It becomes the decisive turning point in each of their lives.

The cost of discipleship

You can tell that there has been a turning point and a change in Naomi's own life, first, by the way she speaks to her daughters-in-law:

> *Go, return each of you to her mother's house. May the LORD deal kindly with you . . . The LORD grant that you may find rest, each of you in the house of her [second] husband.* (1:8-9)

Orpah does go back. But Ruth remains, insisting that she will go with her mother-in-law, despite Naomi's urging, 'Come with me, and nothing is guaranteed. Go back home!'

From one point of view, that is humane advice. But in another sense, Naomi is doing something she could never have done when she and Ruth were living together in the land of Moab. She is talking to her about the cost of belonging to the Lord's covenant people—the cost of discipleship.

Why does Naomi speak of these implications now? Because she wants Ruth to abandon herself to pagan ways? Surely not! She is doing what Jesus would later do when a young ruler asked him: 'What must I do to inherit eternal life?' and Jesus replied, 'Well, there are the commandments: go and obey them.' When the young man said that he had obeyed them all, the Master put him to the test: 'Well now, let me test the truth of that. If you really want to find eternal life, sell everything you own and come and follow me.' That tested him; it revealed a hitherto undetected idol in his heart[9]—for the young man was 'very rich' and went away disheartened.[10] Like Paul, he discovered that the commandment that promised life brought death. Interestingly, in both instances it was the same commandment that proved so significant.

Naomi is doing what she has probably never done, indeed, could not have done, in Moab. She is speaking about what may be involved in yielding to the grace of God. Nothing will be guaranteed to us except that his grace will be sufficient for all our needs, and that he will never be our debtor. There is no promise of financial security, far less material prosperity. God does not guarantee our comfort. That is why the new Naomi is inviting her daughters-in- law to count the cost of belonging to the Lord. It might well mean: no husband; no guaranteed provision or security; no children; no human hope.

Naomi has been changed. When the principles of discipleship were muted in her life in Moab, she could hardly speak clearly about it to her sons or their wives. But now she can speak with integrity—at last.

We are similarly not able to witness with conviction and sincerity to those who ask us about Christ and all that is involved in discipleship when there is little or nothing in our own lives to authenticate what we say to them. But when the Lord restores us and we yield without reservation to him, we can speak with a clear conscience, and assure them:

Fading is the worldling's pleasure,
All his boasted pomp and show;
Solid joys and lasting treasure
None but Zion's children know.[11]

Naomi has come to know this. She is going back to be with the Lord and his people. She will experience his grace. Nothing else ultimately matters. She trusts that God will provide for her needs.

But what about the girls? It is a turning point for Orpah. Presumably, given the marrying age in those days, she is still only in her mid-twenties—an eligible young woman, with the whole of life before her; still with the maternal instinct to bear children, although she is as yet barren. She considers the alternatives:

Jehovah *plus* nothing in Bethlehem
or
everything *minus* Jehovah in Moab.

Orpah makes her decision. She feels more secure with the latter equation and bases her decision on it. She chooses the familiar, the temporal and the visible. Who knows if there is anything more, anyway? She opts for this world's wisdom, and turns away from the wisdom of God.

It is also a turning point for Ruth. 'See, your sister-in-law has gone back to her people and to her gods; return after your sister-in-law,' challenges Naomi. But in verses 16-17 Ruth gives her memorable reply:

> *Do not urge me to leave you or to return from following you. For where you go I will go, and where you lodge I will lodge. Your people shall be my people, and your God my God. Where you die I will die, and there will I be buried. May the LORD do so to me and more also if anything but death parts me from you.*

And then we read: 'And when Naomi saw that she was determined to go with her, she said no more.'

Imagine the scene. Naomi is speaking to Ruth: 'Go back now. Go back now!' But Ruth—is she almost exasperated with her mother-in-law's urging?—eventually gets a word in edgeways: 'Listen! I have been converted. Stop urging me to go back; did you hear me? I have been converted.'

How do we know that? Because what she says is Bible language for Old Testament conversion.

Covenant language

The words at the centre of Ruth's statement are the jewel in the crown of verses 16 and 17 and of the whole chapter: 'Your people shall be my people, and your God my God.' If you are familiar with the language of the Old Testament, these words will ring bells in your memory, even if you are not quite certain why they seem so familiar. Where have you heard or read them before?

When God made his covenant with his people, he said, 'I will be your God, and you shall be my people' (Leviticus 26:12; see also Genesis 17:7-8; Exodus 6:7). Those are the words with which God committed himself to saving them. What Ruth is saying in response to Naomi, then, is: 'This God, who made his covenant with Abraham, who brought his people out of Egypt in the Exodus, who has promised to provide us with grace and salvation—Naomi, this is my God! That is why I am saying, "Your people shall be my people, and your God my God."'

That this is a narrative of a surprising conversion is further confirmed by the later words of Boaz when he first meets Ruth. The 'gossip' he has heard about her (he has never met her before) is that she has 'come to take refuge' under the wings of 'the LORD, the God of Israel' (Ruth 2:12). To shelter or hide under God's 'wings' is a common Old Testament expression for trusting in him as covenant Lord (cf. Psalm 17:8; 36:7; 57:1; 61:4; 63:7; 91:4).

In the words Paul uses to describe the conversion of the Thessalonians, Ruth has 'turned to God from idols to serve the living and true God' (1 Thessalonians 1:9). Without reservation, with no limitation to her commitment both to the Lord and to the Lord's people, this young woman has indeed been converted.

Why me?

This is the time to stand back for a moment and ask ourselves the question we asked before—Naomi's question, which sometimes becomes our question too: 'Lord, why? And why me?'

In the case of Naomi, part of the answer is one word—in fact, a name: Ruth. Ruth's conversion is part of the explanation for Naomi's pain. That pain and God's purposes have been woven together in a manner eloquently expressed by William Cowper:

Deep in unfathomable mines
Of never-failing skill,
He treasures up his bright designs
And works his sovereign will.[12]

If you came across the first chapter of Ruth lying on the ground, and knew no more about the storyline than what this chapter contains, you might well wonder why the title of the book is Ruth. For this first chapter seems to be mainly centred on Naomi. Why does she feature so largely in the opening chapter of a book called *Ruth?* It is because the story of Naomi is about Ruth; or, more accurately, it is about God bringing Ruth to himself and positioning her life in the ongoing unfolding of his purposes for the world.

This is one reason why we can never say that there is a simple equation in Naomi's life: 'She sinned, therefore she is suffering.' God's ultimate purpose has not been to punish her for her family's spiritual failures in abandoning the land and the promises. Rather, through the mysterious intermingling of his providential control over history with Naomi's family's failures, the Lord's purpose has been to reach through her life to bring Ruth to himself.

During Naomi's extended stay in Moab God was ploughing. Now it is time for harvest to begin; now God is beginning to reap.

Homecoming

The third scene in the first chapter is set in Bethlehem. It is now harvest time, the time for reaping.

Here, again, we ought to pause to learn another lesson about biblical narratives in general. They were originally *heard* rather than read. (Even when they had been committed to writing, people could not afford to possess scrolls themselves and presumably many people could not read.) The first hearers were not able to turn back a few pages to remind themselves of earlier details. So at significant points in the development of the plot, biblical narratives throw out hints of what is yet to come. Then these hints are picked up and worked out again.

One such hint comes at the end of the first chapter. It tells us that when the two women return, and Naomi has made her great confession, they arrive in Bethlehem as the barley harvest is beginning (v.22). This is not merely a statement about the time of year. Ruth chapter 1 opened with a famine beginning; it now closes with a harvest beginning. Get the message? The physical famine also marked a time of spiritual famine in Naomi's life. When we are told that harvest time is now beginning, are we being given a hint that we are also on the verge of a spiritual harvest of God's grace in Naomi and Ruth? Have ploughing and sowing given way to reaping?

There are also hints that God's work is much broader than the work he is doing in Naomi and Ruth. Their return seems to have acted as a catalyst for new spiritual stirrings in Bethlehem. The whole town is speaking about them. 'Is this Naomi? What's changed her?'

A few grey hairs perhaps? That would have changed her; the lines of sorrow on her face would have changed her. But the most impressive change in Naomi is her testimony. This woman left 'full' and now she has come back 'empty'. 'There were four of us—and I had three men to support and protect me. We were going to make it on our own. But now you see me. I know now that I cannot find lasting blessing without trusting in the Lord.' Now she comes back humbly.

Naomi does not mean that she went away full in the material sense, since there was a famine. No, she had her full family, with their determination to do for themselves what God would not do for the impenitent. They were not materially full, but full of themselves and their own plans and what they would accomplish. Now she says: 'The LORD [Yahweh[13]] has brought me back empty. Do not call me Naomi ('Pleasant') any longer. Call me by the name Mara ('Bitter'), that my life may be a standing testimony to the way in which God brings the sweet out of the bitter, and gives his grace in the midst of our sin and failure.

No wonder the whole town is 'stirred' (v.19). It is buzzing with the news (the precise translation of the Hebrew verb is debated, but this is certainly its general meaning). Later we discover that even Boaz has heard the local gossip about the Lord's work in these two women's lives. He seems to have been the kind of man who keeps himself scrupulously free from the small-town gossip that may have characterised some of the women of Bethlehem. But even he has heard that Naomi has come back, bringing with her a Moabitess who has been converted. 'You are the girl who has been converted' is the essential meaning of his later words to her in Ruth 2:11-12:

> *All that you have done . . . has been fully told to me . . . a full reward be given you by the LORD, the God of Israel, under whose wings you have come to take refuge.*

The whole town is indeed stirred. There is at least the potential for a deeper spiritual awakening, a cleansing and renewal.

When, over an extended period of time, a church sees no one coming to faith and joining the fellowship, a spiritual torpor often sets in. We say we believe in the potential power of God, but lose faith in his actual power. And so our prayers are faithless and pessimistic. Our church life becomes in-turned. If our congregation is numerically relatively strong, we become narcissistic and self-satisfied. But the truth is that we need an in-breaking of God's grace and power.

It takes only one conversion for a church to begin to believe again in the regenerating power of God. The impact of one individual coming to faith can transform the whole community. God's people begin to believe in conversion again, to pray for God to grant it, and to rejoice that he is at work among them. The ripple effect of God's divine purposes as he touches others is wonderful. Yes, God is still working his purposes out.

And the amazing thing (as we shall see in the rest of the book of Ruth) is that these women, and specially Ruth, discover exactly what Jesus later promised Simon Peter when he said:

> *Truly, I say to you, there is no one who has left house or wife or brothers or parents or children, for the sake of the kingdom of God, who will not receive many times more in this time, and in the age to come eternal life.* (Luke 18:29-30)

The following three chapters of Ruth tell a story of harvest. They show us how God almost systematically replaces everything that Naomi and Ruth have lost.

Looking back from Bethlehem

There is one further thing we must do before we leave the first chapter, and that is to stand back from it and ask ourselves how the divine signature is written into it.

Here is Naomi. Into her life comes the death of her husband Elimelech, then of her son Mahlon, followed by the death of her son Chilion. Yet through death comes the new spiritual life of this young woman Ruth, and the outworking of God's gracious love and purposes.

Where and how do we see the autograph of our Lord Jesus written into this?

Paul sheds light on this in words that provide a key to his own fruitfulness in Christian service. He was:

> *always carrying in the body the death [literally: the dying] of Jesus, so that the life of Jesus may also be manifested in our bodies. For we who live are always being given over to death for Jesus' sake, so that the life of Jesus also may be manifested in our mortal flesh. So death is at work in us, but life in you.* (2 Corinthians 4:10-12)

It is a gospel secret that death is the way to life.

How, and when did Paul learn that? The seed of it was sown in his life on the day when he watched Stephen being stoned to death, apparently pointlessly—the apparent waste of the finest fruit of the gospel in Jerusalem. What is the explanation for this?

Luke constructs the story of the Acts of the Apostles so that we will notice that Stephen's death is intimately related to the new life of Saul of Tarsus. Death-producing-life was a principle written into the warp and woof of his conversion and became the ground plan and blueprint for his own service. Thus the suffering and death of Stephen do have an explanation: Saul of Tarsus is the explanation. Death worked in Stephen: life worked in Saul. Just so, death worked in Naomi, and new life worked in Ruth.

There is much more to come. Will there be an answer to Naomi's prayer—'May the LORD show kindness to you, as you have shown to your dead and to me. May the LORD grant that each of you will find rest in the home of another husband' (1:8, NIV)? But for now the important thing is to recognise the signature of God.

Do you see God's autograph written into your own life? Why are we called to fill up what is still lacking in our fellowship in the sufferings of Jesus (cf. Colossians 1:24)? The answer may lie partly in your own life, and your growth in Christlikeness and maturity. But it is unlikely to lie there exclusively. A large part of it may lie in someone else's life.

Do you ever wonder why some Christians go through the things they experience when there seems to be no reason why they should suffer as they do? God, in his sovereign purpose, may well be using their suffering to bring others to find Christ. Their suffering will bear fruit that will last for ever. Not always from our point of view, but certainly from his.

His purposes will ripen fast,
Unfolding every hour;
The bud may have a bitter taste,
But sweet will be the flower.[14]

Naomi's and Ruth's story well illustrates the words of another barren woman who lived by faith—Hannah, the mother of Samuel:

The LORD kills and brings to life;
he brings down to Sheol and raises up.
The LORD makes poor and makes rich;
he brings low and he exalts.
He raises up the poor from the dust;
he lifts the needy from the ash heap
to make them sit with princes
and inherit a seat of honour.
For the pillars of the earth are the LORD's,
and on them he has set the world.
(1 Samuel 2:6-8)

Ruth 2: 1-23

NOW Naomi had a relative of her husband's, a worthy man of the
clan of Elimelech, whose name was Boaz. [2]And Ruth the Moabite said
to Naomi, 'Let me go to the field and glean among the ears of grain
after him in whose sight I shall find favour.' And she said to her, 'Go, my
daughter.' [3] So she set out and went and gleaned in the field after the
reapers, and she happened to come to the part of the field belonging
to Boaz, who was of the clan of Elimelech. [4]And behold, Boaz came
from Bethlehem. And he said to the reapers, 'The LORD be with you!'
And they answered, 'The LORD bless you.' [5]Then Boaz said to his young
man who was in charge of the reapers, 'Whose young woman is this?'
[6]And the servant who was in charge of the reapers answered, 'She is
the young Moabite woman, who came back with Naomi from the
country of Moab. [7]She said, "Please let me glean and gather among the
sheaves after the reapers." So she came, and she has continued from
early morning until now, except for a short rest.'

[8]Then Boaz said to Ruth, 'Now, listen, my daughter, do not go to glean
in another field or leave this one, but keep close to my young women.
[9]Let your eyes be on the field that they are reaping, and go after them.
Have I not charged the young men not to touch you? And when you are
thirsty, go to the vessels and drink what the young men have drawn.'
[10]Then she fell on her face, bowing to the ground, and said to him, 'Why
have I found favour in your eyes, that you should take notice of me,
since I am a foreigner?' [11]But Boaz answered her, 'All that you have done
for your mother-in-law since the death of your husband has been fully
told to me, and how you left your father and mother and your native
land and came to a people that you did not know before. [12]The LORD
repay you for what you have done, and a full reward be given you by
the LORD, the God of Israel, under whose wings you have come to take

refuge!' 13Then she said, 'I have found favour in your eyes, my lord, for you have comforted me and spoken kindly to your servant, though I am not one of your servants.'

14And at mealtime Boaz said to her, 'Come here and eat some bread and dip your morsel in the wine.' So she sat beside the reapers, and he passed to her roasted grain. And she ate until she was satisfied, and she had some left over. 15When she rose to glean, Boaz instructed his young men, saying, 'Let her glean even among the sheaves, and do not reproach her. 16And also pull out some from the bundles for her and leave it for her to glean, and do not rebuke her.'

17So she gleaned in the field until evening. Then she beat out what she had gleaned, and it was about an ephah of barley. 18And she took it up and went into the city. Her mother-in-law saw what she had gleaned. She also brought out and gave her what food she had left over after being satisfied. 19And her mother-in-law said to her, 'Where did you glean today? And where have you worked? Blessed be the man who took notice of you.' So she told her mother-in-law with whom she had worked and said, 'The man's name with whom I worked today is Boaz.' 20And Naomi said to her daughter-in-law, 'May he be blessed by the LORD, whose kindness has not forsaken the living or the dead!' Naomi also said to her, 'The man is a close relative of ours, one of our redeemers.' 21And Ruth the Moabite said, 'Besides, he said to me, "You shall keep close by my young men until they have finished all my harvest."' 22And Naomi said to Ruth, her daughter-in-law, 'It is good, my daughter, that you go out with his young women, lest in another field you be assaulted.' 23So she kept close to the young women of Boaz, gleaning until the end of the barley and wheat harvests. And she lived with her mother-in-law.

Chapter Three
Boaz: the proper man

'Blessed is the man
who walks not in the counsel of the wicked,
nor stands in the way of sinners,
nor sits in the seat of scoffers;
but his delight is in the law of the LORD,
and on his law he meditates day and night.
He is like a tree
planted by streams of water
that yields its fruit in its season,
and its leaf does not wither.
In all that he does, he prospers.'
(Psalm 1:1-3)

For the first fifteen years of my life my family did not attend church, although my parents considered it part of a 'decent upbringing' to send me to a Sunday school. It was some time after the beginnings of my own conscious faith that they became church-attenders and then members. Partly because of that, I first met some parts of the Bible in unexpected places. That, as it happens, is true of the book of Ruth. Not in the pages of the Old Testament but in a popular Scottish magazine to which my mother subscribed was where I first read the most famous words in the whole book.

We had relatively few books in our home, but our family made much use of the local library. In addition, as an avid reader, I would read every piece of literature that came into the house, not stopping short of the weekly magazine to which my mother subscribed, and that despite the fact that the stories tended to be—at least for a seven-year-old's taste—of an overly romantic kind!

One magazine (it was, and still is, called *The People's Friend*) could still, in the culture of Scotland in the mid- 1950s, include romantic tales involving young ministers going to their first pastoral charges where the choir stalls soon filled with a band of 'hopefuls' (sometimes press-ganged into singing by their even more hopeful mothers!). The titles of some of these stories stuck with me more than the contents—'Where you go I will go'; 'Let nothing separate me from you'. I did not realise that these words were echoes of the Romance of Ruth.

There is no doubt that the book of Ruth contains one of the great romantic narratives in all human literature. But as we have seen, those words spoken to Naomi do not express human devotion alone. At their heart lies Ruth's confession that she has begun to experience God's covenant grace, his *hesed*: Your people shall be my people, and your God my God' is the reason she says, 'Where you go I will go . . .'

The covenant-keeping God

Thus, the author of Ruth establishes early on that this book is not merely about human relationships but about the great covenant-making and covenant-keeping Lord God and the way in which he brings us to faith. Then, as the providence of God continues to work, we recognise the fulfilment of a promise of Jesus: as the Lord's people yield everything to him, they discover in the process, in different ways, that God is never their debtor.

We are given a hint of this already in Ruth 1. Although Naomi left Bethlehem 'full' and has now come back 'empty', she returned to the Promised Land with her daughter-in-law soon after the Lord visited his people and just as the harvest was beginning.

Naomi, as we have seen, has prayed for Ruth, and for the Lord's blessing upon her life. As Bible readers, we are invited now to have an eagle eye and to be on the look-out for the way God will respond to that prayer. We are encouraged to ask: If God is the hearer and the answerer of prayer, if he keeps his covenant promises, will the prayer in Ruth 1:8-9 be answered? Will the Lord open his hand to satisfy the needs of these women?

So, just as the opening chapter begins with a hint of how the first part of the drama will develop, the second chapter does the same.

Points of view

Two things help us to appreciate and enjoy what is going on in this narrative.

Splitting the screen

Ancient storytellers did not have the benefit of italics or underlining. So they found other ways of highlighting the details of their narratives in order to draw their hearers or readers into the emotions of the drama. This explains why biblical narratives, particularly Old Testament ones, sometimes contain details that at first sight may seem redundant. If the author tells you something that you could learn in any case from the story itself, he almost certainly wants you to focus on it, and to ask: Why is this being highlighted? How will this piece of information prove to be significant in the outworking of God's sovereign providences? Redundancy, at least in biblical narratives, is often repetition for the sake of emphasis.

That is certainly true of Ruth 2:1:

> *Now Naomi had a relative of her husband's, a worthy man of the clan of Elimelech, whose name was Boaz.*

All of this we will learn in the course of the narrative. Why draw attention to it now? The narrator is saying to us: Keep your eye fixed upon Boaz, because it may be (as a good author he does not tell you yet that it will be), that *he* is God's answer to Naomi's prayer—possibly in ways you would not expect, and certainly these women would never expect. After all, the Old Testament God is the New Testament God who 'is able to do far more abundantly than all that we ask or think' (Ephesians 3:20).

But why are we told this? Because this narrative proceeds at two different levels.

In order to give us a sense of how God effects his providential purposes, Bible narratives sometimes use the literary equivalent of a movie maker's or television director's 'split screen' technique. They do with words what modern technology can do visually—splitting the screen so that we have two different perspectives simultaneously or can compare two different actions or events, and relate them to each other. If you read Scripture narrative with that 'technique' in mind, you will notice how often Bible writers use it; not to make a sporting occasion appear more exciting and dramatic, but to give us an important insight into the nature of God's working.

When this split screen technique is used, we are being encouraged to read the narrative from two different points of view: the human and the divine, the 'accidents' of history and the activity of God's sovereignty. The opening words of the book of Daniel are a good example:

> *In the third year of the reign of Jehoiakim king of Judah, Nebuchadnezzar king of Babylon came to Jerusalem and besieged it. And the Lord gave Jehoiakim king of Judah into his hand, with some of the vessels of the house of God. (Daniel 1:1-2)*

Man proposes, but it is God who disposes. Nebuchadnezzar conquers, but only because of the purposes of the Lord.

Thus, one point of view is that of the participants in the drama. They have little or no knowledge of what God is doing in and through their lives. They cannot see the end from the beginning. They may know that God is sovereign, but they have no idea how he will demonstrate his sovereignty. That is the position we ordinarily occupy in our own lives. We do not have direct access to the mind of God to know the details of his plans and purposes.

Here in Ruth this narrative technique appears in a wonderfully unselfconscious way. While the narrator knows much more clearly than the characters what God is doing, he refers to God only twice, while they mention him over twenty times! Thus he brilliantly underlines that while the presence of God is real to Naomi, Ruth and Boaz, his purposes remain hidden.

But then there is another perspective: the narrator knows what God is doing because he can look backwards from the vantage point of the conclusion of the story, or at least from its interim conclusion. He can see the footprints of God running through the narrative; he can see the trajectory of what God is doing in order to fulfil his purposes.

There is an additional perspective that Christians can enjoy as they read the Old Testament. In one sense, we are able to see even further than the original author because we can place his narrative in the context of its ultimate fulfillment in the coming of Jesus Christ. We not only have the human point of view and the divine point of view, but also the trajectory of God's working stretching beyond these events in the Old Testament towards their fulfilment in Jesus Christ.

We, too, are involved in the drama of God's unfolding purposes. Frequently we cannot understand what God is doing. But in the Scriptures God is saying to us, as he said to John in the book of Revelation: Come up here to this vantage point for a moment and see what I am doing (Revelation 4:1ff.)! It is as if the Bible as a whole is saying: Come up here and see how God is on his throne, working out his perfect purposes; and view things in your own life and times from his point of view.

The divine autograph

Here, then, in the book of Ruth, we learn a lesson in looking at things from God's point of view. We are taught what kind of God he is. We are told: This is the handwriting he uses to write his autograph. These are its distinctive features. Look out for the way he writes his signature in your life, too.

Scripture sheds divine light on the darkness of our lives not because we have the ability to interpret the movements of God, but because his Word gives us wisdom. It is a lamp to us (Psalm 119:105). It illumines our understanding of God's ways. Thus, when we are in this or that situation, feeling our way in the darkness, not able to see his hand, trace his design, or interpret his purposes, we nevertheless know the kind of thing he does, and we know the kind of God he is. In this way we learn Isaiah's lesson:

Who among you fears the LORD
and obeys the voice of his servant?
Let him who walks in darkness
and has no light
trust in the name of the LORD
and rely on his God.
(Isaiah 50:10)

We trust the Lord because he is the God of Abraham, Isaac and Jacob, the great patriarchs, and the God of the apostles, and the

God and Father of our Lord Jesus Christ. But we also know we can trust him because he is the God who has done marvellous things in the lives of very ordinary people. Thus, in Scripture God writes in block capital letters the principles of his providence so that when he rewrites them in our lives in small, sometimes microscopic, writing, we see that he is the same God. He uses the same handwriting, and displays the same providential care for our lives as in the lives recorded in Scripture.

Happenstances happen

That leads to a further feature worth noting about the narrative in chapter 2. The author writes: 'Ruth the Moabite said to Naomi, "Let me go to the field and glean."' Then he goes on to say in verse 3:

> *So she set out and went and gleaned in the field after the reapers, and she happened to come to the part of the field belonging to Boaz, who was of the clan of Elimelech.*

That is a somewhat sanitised version of what the author actually wrote. More literally translated, the words are something like this: 'the happenstance that happened to her was . . .'

Have you ever casually remarked to a fellow Christian, 'You know, when I was doing this, it just happened that . . .', only to receive the pious (and critical) rebuke: 'But nothing just happens!'? How unspiritual you are made to look! But the author of the book of Ruth is comfortable writing in this way. Of course we know that there are no 'happenstances'. So does the author of Ruth—which is why, in this instance, a literal translation helps us to enjoy the narrative the way he intends! He wants us to sit up and take notice.

Can you imagine yourself seated round a campfire listening to this story? Do you not see a little smile playing on the lips of the narrator? He knows that nothing 'just happens'; we know that nothing 'just happens'. But he also knows that, like Ruth, our understanding and appreciation of the ways of God and our ability to guess what he is going to do are very limited indeed. As the theologians put it in succinct fashion, events that are certain to God are unpredictable and contingent from our point of view. There are many things in our lives that seem to 'happen' to us by happenstance, things that we may never understand.

From Ruth's point of view things do 'just happen'. She has no idea about the significance of gleaning in Boaz's field. She probably does not even know who Boaz is! She certainly does not know where God is providentially leading her. The providences of God, as John Flavel cleverly put it, are like Hebrew words: they can only be read properly backwards.

A question of perspective

Here, then, the author is helping us to view our lives as though they were being played out on a split screen on which we see both the sovereignty of God and his lordship over all the details of our lives, and also the contingency or unpredictability of the events of the world in which we live. From a human point of view, everything could be quite different from the way it is.

Yet at the same time we recognise that in the midst of our confusion and the happenstances and surprises of life there is a sovereign God in heaven whose hand is upon us every moment of the day, a God who reigns over every inch of the universe in which we live. So we know that nothing 'just happens'. Not even a sparrow falls to the ground without his knowledge, interest and rule (Matthew 10:29). All things come to pass under the sovereign wisdom and purpose of our heavenly Father, working together for the good of those who love him, who are called according to his purpose (Romans 8:28).

That is why we can be quietly confident—not because we know exactly what God is doing in this unpredictable world, but because we know that what is unpredictable to us is already predicted by him. He has written his purposes for us in his own book, and numbered our days before one of them was given birth or saw the light of day (Psalm 139:16).

Off to glean

Against that background, the narrative proceeds. Ruth goes out into the fields to glean. She is a woman who rolls up her sleeves and gets on with the business of living. 'Let me go to the field and glean among the ears of grain after him in whose sight I shall find *favour.*' This last word is immensely significant—because it echoes Naomi's prayer in chapter 1, verse 8: 'May the LORD deal *kindly* with you.' In both instances, the Hebrew word *hesed* is used. There is a deliberate echo here of the attribute of God that the book of Ruth constantly emphasises: his grace, his kindness, his covenant favour, his faithful love.

God had made a law about gleaning. It was an expression of his love and concern for the poor, the stranger and the marginalised—a concern that he commanded his people to share. The Torah enjoined those who had farms not to harvest their fields so as to exhaust the crop. Instead, they were to leave a border around each field where the poor and the needy could come to glean for themselves (see Leviticus 19:9-10; 23:22). Thus, everyone within the compass of God's covenant, both 'the haves' and 'the havenots', might be fed. This was the law of grace, the rule of the bountiful Father. Grace and graciousness were written into the commandments he had given his people.

So Ruth goes out into the fields with her mother-in-law's blessing: 'Go, my daughter' (2:2). It *just so happens* that she finds herself working in a field belonging to Boaz, a member of her deceased father-in-law's family or clan (2:3), and 'Just then Boaz arrived', as the New International Version renders the opening words of 2:4. The English Standard Version, with the older versions, catches the more graphic intention of the author: 'Behold, Boaz . . .'. This is not merely old-fashioned language. The author is saying, 'Look! Do you see what is happening? Keep your eyes glued to this man! It "so happens" that Ruth is gleaning in the field of Boaz. And just at that time Boaz himself "just happens" to appear.'

Coincidence? Hardly.

A foreman and a foreigner

Boaz engages in two conversations: the first is with his foreman; the second is an extended interchange with Ruth. In conversation with his foreman, Boaz learns something about this young woman whom he has apparently already noticed, and about whom he already knows something. And in the second conversation he addresses Ruth specifically and directly.

It is fascinating to notice what happens. Having greeted his harvesters, Boaz asks the foreman, 'Whose young woman is this?' *Whose* young woman? The foreman replies (notice carefully the way he describes Ruth): 'She is the young Moabite woman, who came back with Naomi from the country of Moab. She said, "Please let me glean and gather among the sheaves after the reapers"' (2:6). The foreman then continues: 'She went into the field and has worked steadily from morning till now, except for a short rest in the shelter' (2:7 NIV).

Some commentators read the foreman as saying, not that Ruth has been 'working steadily' in the field, but, 'She has been standing here from morning until now.' Ruth is then no quiet, mousy lady. 'Believe me,' says the foreman, 'she has been standing here for hours, refusing to budge until she speaks to you. She wants to glean in your field, and won't take no for an answer.'

It is more likely that the standard translations best express the intention of the author: what Ruth continues to do is not stand but glean. She has asked permission to glean; she goes into the field; she works steadily until Boaz arrives. In either case, persistence, stickability, is her hallmark. In any case, she has no knowledge (as yet) that this is the field of a redeemer. So far only we, the readers, know this.

Boaz then engages Ruth in a remarkable conversation that will lead to her material blessing and that will also supply Naomi's physical needs. But it also hints at a deeper, more lasting supply of love:

> *Now, listen, my daughter, do not go to glean in another field or leave this one, but keep close to my young women. Let your eyes be on the field that they are reaping, and go after them. Have I not charged the young men not to touch you? And when you are thirsty, go to the vessels and drink what the young men have drawn.* (Ruth 2:8-9)

Later, Boaz discreetly displays his affection:

> *Boaz said to her, 'Come here and eat some bread and dip your morsel in the wine.' So she sat beside the reapers, and he passed to her roasted grain. And she ate until she was satisfied, and she had some left over. When she rose to glean, Boaz instructed his young men, saying, 'Let her glean even among the sheaves, and do not reproach her. And also pull out some from the bundles for her and leave it for her to glean, and do not rebuke her.'* (Ruth 2:14-16)

Bread, wine, roasted grain, protection, provision—is this a burgeoning romance, or are we reading too much into Boaz's words? In all likelihood that is exactly the tantalizing question the narrator intends to plant into our minds! But look at the marvellous ending to this passage:

> *So she gleaned in the field until evening. Then she beat out what she had gleaned, and it was about an ephah of barley. And she took it up and went into the city. Her mother-in-law saw what she had gleaned. She also brought out and gave her what food she had left over after being satisfied. (Ruth 2:17-18)*

Picture the superabundant supply that Boaz's field—and therefore Boaz—has provided. Ruth goes home with, in one hand, a 'doggy bag' left over from her lunch, but also, as we are told towards the end of the passage, with an ephah— some thirty pounds—of threshed barley. When did you last carry a thirty-pound sack of potatoes from the supermarket to the car (far less to your home!)—without a trolley?

Perhaps in the days of the judges women did a good deal more weight training than is normal today! But it is also possible that while the details are historically reliable, the author's real purpose is to give us a moment of light relief from the heightening emotion of his story. Most of us can sustain tension only so long. We need a moment or two to relax. Perhaps, then, we are meant to enjoy a quiet smile at this scene. Here is the young widow who emigrated with probably little more than the clothes on her back. That morning she left the bare cupboards in the home of her Jewish mother-in-law. Now, only hours later, she staggers home with thirty pounds of grain over her shoulders! It is hardly surprising that Naomi asks her, perhaps breathlessly, 'Where did you go today? Where did you work? Blessed be the man who took notice of you!'

But if we are now meant to smile at Naomi's astonishment—for we already know the answer, and we feel sure that the story of God's plans is still unravelling—we are also meant to see how the theme of the first chapter has developed.

Chapter 1 ended with Naomi's confession that she left 'full' but has returned to the land of promise 'empty'. She was emptied because of sin. God also substantially emptied her of her spirit of self-reliance. His purpose was that she might be filled with the provision hidden within the divine plan.

This story is like a great orchestral symphony. Motifs from the overture are picked up and worked out in the later movements. Already we, the audience, are meant to recognize a theme running throughout this narrative. God is saying to us: 'Do you see what I do with my children when they trust in me, when, like Ruth, they have said to me, "You are my God and your people will be my people"? I never remain their debtor. I send the full empty away, but those who are empty I fill with good things.'[15]

Here is a young woman who left everything behind. One morning she leaves her mother-in-law for the day. But in the evening she returns home, not only full, but staggering under the weight of God's blessing and provision. The great reversal has begun!

The meaning of *hesed*

We have now developed both an empathy with, and a new appreciation for, Naomi (although perhaps she ought not yet to be trusted absolutely; as we shall see, her faith is not yet anxiety-free). Her prayer in chapter 1 is, in a sense, the key to what is taking place in chapter 2. Further, she puts her finger on exactly what is happening in this narrative when she says about Boaz: 'May he be blessed by the LORD, whose kindness [Hebrew: *hesed,* covenant love] has not forsaken the living or the dead!' (2:20).

Blessing, as Naomi well knows, is the expression of God's covenant goodness to those who trust and obey him, who mirror his image and express his character in the way in which they live in this world. The Lord has shown *hesed*; Boaz has also shown *hesed*.[16] Then Naomi adds something that *we* already know, but Ruth does not. She says (Is there a coy look on her face?), 'The man is a close relative of ours, one of our redeemers.'

Do you think that in Naomi's words there is just a little hint that she is being tempted to take things into her own hands? Naomi is, perhaps, like a mother straight out of those old *People's Friend* magazines. Had Boaz been a new young minister, Naomi's widowed daughter-in-law would soon be in the choir, sitting in full view of the pulpit!

Yet at the same time, Naomi puts her finger on the theology of what is happening here. This is *hesed,* one of the 'big' words in the Old Testament Scriptures. It appears around 250 times, and dominantly with reference to God himself. He is a God of loving-kindness—as the beautiful old English of the Authorised Version has it. When God revealed himself to Moses, he said that he was a God full of *hesed* (Exodus 34:6)—not simply love or kindness in an ordinary sense. It means God's deep goodness expressed in his covenant commitment, his absolute loyalty, his obligating of himself to bring to fruition the blessings that he has promised, *whatever it may cost him personally to do that.*

This covenanted commitment is a central theme in the Old Testament and forms the melody line of the book of Ruth.

Covenant blessing

At the heart of the Old Testament lies the covenant that God made with Abraham, Isaac and Jacob, which was continued in the covenant made with the people through Moses (Exodus 6:2-5). In it God pledged himself to them: 'I will be your God and you will be my people.' This covenant is not an agreement reached by two parties as the result of protracted negotiations. It is a divine promise, confirmed by God's oath and sealed with a physical sign. It is unilateral (one-sided) in its *origin.* God sovereignly and graciously binds himself to us in his covenant, and binds himself to fulfil all that is promised in it. But it is bilateral (two-sided) in its *outworking.* God promises that as his people respond to him in faithfulness, he will shower his blessings on them. But should they respond in disobedience, they will experience the darkness of his curse.

The life of faith in the Old Testament is set within this framework. Later, in the New Testament, the book of Hebrews indicates that the same dynamic is present in the new covenant in Christ.[17] Our God is a covenant-making, covenant-keeping God. As we live responding to his promises, he showers his blessings upon us. If we should persist in unfaithfulness and disobedience, we will experience the darkness of his judgement curse. Thus, even although the children of Israel were his own people, when they proved to be persistently disobedient they fell under his judgement and were eventually exiled from the covenant land.[18]

When we see the word 'bless' in the Bible, then, it means very much more than we mean when we say to someone who has sneezed, 'Bless you.' Think, for example, of Paul's words: 'Blessed be the God . . . who has blessed us in Christ with every spiritual blessing in the heavenly places' (Ephesians 1:3). Paul means that in Christ Jesus the covenant blessings promised to Abraham have been showered upon us.

Jesus, who was faithful to God's covenant, bore the curse appropriate to our faithlessness and disobedience to it in order that God's blessing might be ours:

> *Christ redeemed us from the curse of the law by becoming a curse for us—for it is written, "Cursed is everyone who*

> *is hanged on a tree"—so that in Christ Jesus the blessing of Abraham might come to the Gentiles, so that we might receive the promised Spirit through faith.* (*Galatians 3:13-14*)

God's *hesed,* his loving-kindness, has been poured out upon us. He has been loyal to his covenant promise, whatever the cost to himself—*even when that cost was the death of his Son.*

It was for this—with an audacity he could not begin to grasp, but with a boldness encouraged by his covenant keeping God—that David, the adulterer, schemer and murderer, had prayed when he cried: 'Have mercy on me, O God, according to your steadfast love [*hesed*] . . . blot out my transgressions' (Psalm 51:1). David could not have realised that he was, in fact, ultimately praying for Christ to die for him, to deal with his blood guiltiness (Psalm 51:14). Yet he knew enough to realise how '*Blessed* is the man whose transgression is forgiven . . . *Blessed* is the man against whom the LORD counts no iniquity' (Psalm 32:1-2). He had been delivered from the curse of the covenant and tasted its blessing.

In fact, there is still an echo of this biblical background when we say, 'Bless you' to someone who sneezes. The origin of the expression lies in the terrible plagues that swept Europe during the Middle Ages and decimated the population. The plague was seen as a divine curse, and sneezing one of the symptoms of having caught the dreaded disease; hence the line in the children's rhyming game:

> *Ring a ring o' roses, a pocket full o' posies:*
> *Atishoo! Atishoo! We all fall down.*

The prayer (for it was a prayer), '[May God] bless you', originally meant, 'May the curse be turned from you; may you instead know God's blessing of life' ('fall down' in the rhyme being a euphemism for dying!).

So when Naomi says that Boaz has not abandoned *hesed,* covenant loyalty, God's loyal love, his through-and through goodness, it is as though the narrator is saying to us: 'Stop there! Think about that! See what is really happening in these events. Don't you see that these events demonstrate the heavenly Father's steadfast love and kindness as he works in the lives of his children?'

When she left Moab, Naomi told her two daughters-in-law to return to their mothers' houses, and prayed, 'May the LORD deal kindly [*hesed*] with you . . .' (1:8). Orpah had turned away from the prospect of that covenant love and blessing, whereas Ruth clung to it: 'Your people shall be my people, and your God my God'—I take this covenant. And in fulfilling this covenant the heavenly Father has now begun to shower down upon Ruth the blessings of his own *hesed.*

Will two make one?

Remember that the narrator has invited us to ask the old question, 'Will they or won't they?'We ought not to get so lost in contemplating the glories of God's providence that we fail to see the beginnings of a divinely given romance here! Naomi's prayer has hinted at it; the introduction of Boaz has given us another clue. We know, or at least suspect, how this story will end. But like the stories we loved to hear again and again in childhood, the pleasure of this one lies partly in spotting the clues. For our narrator is giving us hints and clues not only about what will happen, but about why it is so appropriate for it to happen.

What we have here is, in one sense, a rewriting of the first romance recorded in Genesis 2:20-24[19]

> *The man gave names to all livestock and to the birds of the heavens and to every beast of the field. But for Adam there*

was not found a helper fit for him. So the LORD God caused a deep sleep to fall upon the man, and while he slept took one of his ribs and closed up its place with flesh. And the rib that the Lord God had taken from the man he made into a woman and brought her to the man. Then the man said, 'This at last is bone of my bones and flesh of my flesh; she shall be called Woman, because she was taken out of Man.' Therefore a man shall leave his father and his mother and hold fast to his wife, and they shall become one flesh.

This time, however, it is set in a fallen world, where the obstacles to it are complex.

Boaz is a man who is alone. His words to Ruth convey a certain pathos—he knows it is not good for him to be alone. But this time God goes not into the man's rib-cage but into 'the far country' in order to bring to him the woman he has made for him, who is really suitable for him.[20] We shall see a further echo of this in the next chapter when, Adam-like, Boaz awakens from sleep to find Ruth, who is to be his own Eve![21]

So several things are going on in this passage simultaneously. There is the general principle that the loving loyalty of the Lord manifests itself in the loving loyalty of Boaz and Ruth. But there is also a further dimension to the narrative. If it is true that written into it is a kind of rerunning of the Garden of Eden, but in a fallen world, then it may provide guidance for those who are contemplating marriage. By what means should we expect to be awakened to say, 'God has brought me to see that this is the person who is suited for me'?

And then for those who are married, this is a marvelous illustration of the loyalty love to which God calls us in marriage. For godliness in married life is essentially a matter of being like God, not by becoming superman or superwoman, but by being a husband or wife who displays the *hesed*, the deep goodness of a loyal love that is committed to blessing one's marriage partner, no matter what the expense to oneself.

How is *hesed* seen in Ruth?

This covenant loyalty and kindness is the first thing that attracts Boaz's attention, even before he sees or meets Ruth. He knows that she has taken the covenant for herself, Moabitess though she is. And he has heard of the fruit of her faith in the *hesed* she has displayed:

> *All that you have done for your mother-in-law since the death of your husband has been fully told to me, and how you left your father and mother and your native land and came to a people that you did not know before.* (2:11)

In essence, Boaz is saying: 'I have heard that you are a godly woman, and that God's love and loyalty are already manifested in your life.'

This *hesed* is displayed in Ruth in a number of other ways.

A meek and quiet spirit

First of all, it is evident in what Peter would later call the 'gentle and quiet spirit' that is the hallmark of women after God's heart—in a word, meekness:

> *Let your adorning be the hidden person of the heart with the imperishable beauty of a gentle and quiet spirit, which in God's sight is very precious. For this is how the holy women who hoped in God used to adorn themselves, by submitting to their husbands.* (1 Peter 3:4-5)

We must not misunderstand this. The 'holy women' to whom Peter refers in this context were different from each other in personality: some by nature quiet, others by nature extrovert. But in spirit, whatever their personality, they all had these qualities in common: a gentleness and a quiet peace and poise in spirit.

In Ruth's case these qualities are evident in the way in which she responds to harsh providences. She has recognized and submitted to the hand of God in and through them; she has heard and trusted in the covenant word of God. That is what meekness is: submission to God's providence, listening to God's voice—not least when his word cuts across our native desires, and when his providences cut across all our natural longings. Meekness is saying, 'Lord, you have said it, you have done it, and since this is so, I will trust you.' That disposition towards the Lord always demonstrates itself in our relations with others. It recurs when Ruth exclaims: 'Why have I found favour in your eyes, that you should take notice of me, since I am a foreigner?' (Ruth 2:10).

The world around us today cringes at this kind of speech; but it has resisted the grace of God that would humble its pride and make its spirit meek and profoundly grateful for every blessing the Lord extends to it. The times in which we live must rank among the most ungrateful in history—at least in the western world, which seems so largely to have abandoned the gospel of Christ. With what have we replaced it? Agrumbling and complaining generation— that is the fruit of a refusal to acknowledge the grace and favour of God. By contrast, the meek and gentle are appreciative of every touch of God's kindness. And that is what is so characteristic of Ruth.

The grace of law

We see Ruth's meekness in another important way. She seems to think of the rights that are hers under the law of God as privileges given to her by the grace of God.

Ruth recognises what an unbeliever could never recognise. Unbelievers tend to see God's law as an enemy, an expression of God's antagonism (isn't it full of 'thou shalt nots'?). They see the law as given only to *condemn*; they see no grace in law. Not so the believer. For the believer recognises that the God who gave the law is the God of the Exodus, the God of grace, the God who sets his people free to live in the land he gives to them, enjoying the blessings he promised. The Bible teaches that God's law is rooted in his grace. Witness the preface to the Ten Commandments— the commanding God of Sinai is the redeeming God of the Exodus (Exodus 20:1-2).

And this is the same God of whom Paul says:

> *He who did not spare his own Son but gave him up for us all, how will he not also with him graciously give us all things? (Romans 8:32)*

He has given his law in his grace, indeed in his *hesed*, to direct our lives that they may be wholesome and holy and well-pleasing to him. It guides us into the pathway of divine blessing. That is how Ruth sees the law of God in her life. She is grateful for the provision God has made for her through it because she knows that she deserves nothing from his hand.

The meek *inherit* the earth because they see that they possess nothing of their own (Matthew 5:5). They have become poor in spirit and learned to mourn for their sins. Their mouths—to use Paul's dramatic language—have been shut in the presence of the Holy One (Romans 3:19). There is nothing to be said by way of self-defence. 'What becomes of our boasting? It is excluded' (Romans 3:27). But God's *hesed* opens our mouths: we boast in the hope of the glory of God; we boast even in our sufferings; best of all, we have come to boast in God himself (Romans 5:2,3,11)![22]

Ruth does not know the full story of how God's grace will be revealed in Christ. But the pattern of that grace: living under the curse, discovering covenant grace, experiencing God's saving blessings—these are realities to her. She knows, long before David pens the words, that it is the meek who inherit the land of promise (Psalm 37:11). In that she has a foretaste of the way in which this promise will come to greater fulfilment in Christ, when he, the meek one, the true Adam, will inherit the earth and share it with those who are meek.[23] So, in anticipation, Ruth's meekness opens her mouth in gratitude for the *hesed* of the Lord.

A holy consistency

Ruth also displays *hesed* in another way: in the consistency with which she pursues the specific tasks that God, in his providence, has given her. The foreman notices that. A foreman would!

But this foreman may also be—at least in one respect—a contrast to Boaz. Has he risen to his position because he is a stickler for the letter of the law, a man who can be trusted 'to run a tight ship'? Is that why he—presumably an orthodox Jew—is so reticent about pronouncing the young stranger's name—although probably everyone in town knows what it is? 'The young Moabite woman', he calls her (2:6). Not 'Ruth' but 'the Moabite woman'. Yet he knows she came from Moab with Naomi. She has been in his field all day. Perhaps he is embarrassed to let his master know he has allowed her to glean? But are we meant to feel the shiver going up his spine that he, an orthodox Jew, has been speaking to a 'Moabite woman' at all? Nevertheless, the foreman has to concede that Ruth asked permission to glean, and that she has worked steadily since the morning, except for a short rest to shelter from the midday sun. The foreman describes only her activity; but the narrator means us to see her spiritual quality. One of the expressions of God's grace in her life is the way she goes about the duties God has given to her—with a holy consistency!

Grace-produced character

Are we surprised, perhaps even incredulous, that when Boaz comes to his field and sees Ruth gleaning there, he immediately recognises that there is something different about her? We have lost, or certainly almost lost, the conviction that the grace of God produces such quality of character in the lives of his people that simply their presence and demeanour express their experience of God's grace and their commitment to him.

It was not always so. B. B. Warfield, the famous Princeton Seminary theologian, in a telling story he records in his little essay, 'Is the Shorter Catechism Worthwhile?',[24] makes the point that grace-produced character is one of the ways that we 'adorn the doctrine of God our Saviour'.[25] He describes an incident in a western city in nineteenth-century America. In this city, rioting, hubbub and confusion were the order of the day, but in the midst of the confusion, a US army officer noticed a man who had such presence about him that people were staring at him as he walked down the street.

The two men approached one another. Probably both had been taught never to stare at strangers! But as the man passed the army officer, the latter found himself drawn like a magnet to turn round and look at him. To his horror he realised that the other man had also stopped and was now coming towards him. The stranger prodded him on the chest with his forefinger and asked, 'What is the chief end of man?'

Those words form the first and most famous question in the Shorter Catechism—perhaps the best-known and most widely used instruction manual in the history of the Christian church. The army officer was both amazed and relieved! He was a devout Christian and had learned his catechism as a boy. He enthusiastically—and correctly—replied: 'Man's chief end is to glorify God, and to enjoy him for ever.'

Can you guess what the other man said to him? 'I knew you were a Shorter Catechism boy by your looks!' 'Why,' he replied, 'that's exactly what I was thinking about you!' There was just 'something about him', and this was apparent in the most ordinary activities of life, such as walking down a street. The truth of Scripture had transformed his character. As Warfield himself adds, 'It is worth while to be a Shorter Catechism boy. They grow to be men.'[26]

The Lord's people should have 'something' about them; something in the way they talk, and walk, and react, and in the manner in which they live, that expresses the fact that ultimately they are not so much citizens of this world as citizens of heaven (Philippians 3:20).

This lesson was impressed on me on the night my own Christian life really began. That evening I heard a young professional man in Glasgow describe the events that had led him to faith. His story went something like this. As he moved around the office he regularly passed what used to be called a 'typing pool' (yes, this was last century when such places existed!). There were (if I recall correctly) three typewriters in the room, and three typists. He began to notice that one of the typewriters was operated with a consistency that was lacking in the other two. At first this was just an observation he made. But as he repeatedly passed the typing pool, he kept noticing the same thing. It probably was a source of irritation. Eventually he mentioned it to a colleague: 'Every time I pass that typing pool one of those typewriters is going with a consistency that you never hear in the others!'

The other responded casually, 'Oh, that will be (mentioning the girl's name)—she's a Christian.' With that he walked on—leaving the young man standing with now another question! 'What is the connection between the way someone types and the fact that she's a Christian?' Soon he himself became a Christian, too.

It was impressive to hear how the steady march of God's grace had overtaken the young businessman through the faithful witness of a stranger; I thought I could hear similar steps behind me, too. I do not know the identity of that typist. But it has often crossed my mind that, unknown to her, the faith she so consistently expressed in her life became a link in the chain that brought me to faith—a link in the chain that led to my writing (and your reading) this book! And who knows?—since someone may read this book as an outsider to faith—through this book she may become a link in the chain that brings others to faith.

Boaz is putting his finger on the new source of Ruth's life when he says (in yet another significant prayer), 'The LORD repay you for what you have done, and a full reward be given you by the LORD, the God of Israel, under whose wings you have come to take refuge [or, rest]!' (2:12). Refuge and rest were what the Exodus led to; God bore his people on eagles' wings to give them rest (Isaiah 63:14); rest is what Christ came to give us (Matthew 11:28-30). Now, like the psalmist (Psalm 91:1-4), Ruth rests in the covenant loyalty of the Lord, and in turn he reproduces covenant faithfulness in her life. That is a woman worth noticing at any age or stage.

Boaz

But then, of course, there is Boaz. How is the fruit of God's covenant mercy and loving-kindness displayed in him? He fits exactly the description of the godly man in the book of Proverbs, the man who demonstrates covenant loyalty and faithfulness:

Let not steadfast love and faithfulness forsake you;
bind them around your neck;
write them on the tablet of your heart.
So you will find favour and good success

> *in the sight of God and man.*
> *(Proverbs 3:3-4)*

How does that also appear in Boaz? In a number of ways.

A God-centred life

First, in his attitude to the Lord, especially in the evident God-centredness of his life. It is obvious even in the small details—indeed, especially in the small details. We see it as he arrives from Bethlehem and greets the harvesters: 'The LORD [Yahweh, the covenant name for God] be with you!' You can tell by the setting, and by his bearing as the narrative proceeds, that the words are not some cheap platitude. This is a man so centred upon God himself that his chief desire for others is that they should similarly be centred in the blessing of the Lord. He is concerned that it should fall upon those who work with him and for him. His principal concern for his workers is not merely that they provide him with a good harvest but that they may know the Lord and his blessing. Their response indicates the affection and esteem in which he is held.

Boaz exemplifies in Old Testament times the principle that Paul enunciates in the New. Since we no longer know Christ according to the flesh, or judge him by worldly standards, we do not look at others according to the flesh either, or judge them by worldly standards (2 Corinthians 5:16). We think about others from the divine perspective, and we seek for others the divine blessing. What Boaz is praying for his workers here, as he invokes the great covenant name of God, is the benediction of God, which lay at the very heart of the covenant: 'I will be with you as your Lord.' Boaz's heart is taken up with the blessing of God on the lives of others.

Law and love

But there is a further indication of this. Notice Boaz's instinctive attitude to the needy, the marginalised and the poor. This is always the test of a man.

In Boaz law and love are one. Thus, because God is his covenant God, God's law is his way of life. He exemplifies the book of Proverbs. He exemplifies the principles of the first psalm. He exemplifies Torah. He knows the blessing of the Lord because he walks in the way of the Lord.

No detail of God's law is too small for Boaz to put into practice. Love does not ignore the law because it is more important than the law, or act as if it can abandon the law because its nature is to love. Rather, love shows what the intention of the law really is. It is the fulfilment of the law, not the rejection of it (Galatians 5:14). In this case, law's love commands that a proportion of the harvest must be left for the poor and the needy, for the stranger and the oppressed. The margin around the field is to be there so that those who are marginalised in God's field (the Promised Land) might share in the divine benediction of the harvest—which, after all, is the Lord's.

Notice how Boaz interprets this law of love. Not as a man who goes away and does his sums, Pharisee-like, and says, 'Now—how small a margin can I leave (in my fields) in order to make sure that I leave plenty of profit margin (in my bank account)?' Never! Love shows the fullness of the grace of God in the law. In Boaz's hands, the law of God is an instrument to display the riches of the *hesed* of his Lord. He literally heaps blessing on Ruth and Naomi!

So the next stage in the drama sees Ruth with thirty pounds of grain over her shoulder! She comes home to Naomi—perhaps almost dropping at the feet of her mother-in- law after such a back-breaking day of gleaning and carrying. Is she greeted with a 'Where on earth have you been all this time? I've been worrying about you!'? Ruth's reply is surely: 'I met a man who walks in the law of the Lord, and who meditates on it day and night, who has shown me how the law can be the chief delight of a child of God. His tenderheartedness was amazing . . . He spoke kindly to me. He showed *hesed* to us.'

The test of maturity
Why is that so significant? Jesus gives us the answer. The real evidence of character and the ultimate test of spiritual maturity is not how someone reacts to the great, the famous, the rich, and the noble, but how that person has responded to the marginalised, the unnoticed, the poor, the struggler, and the needy. Not who you know, but the needy for whom you care, this is the real measure of men and women. It is certainly the real measure of those who serve Christ. The criteria are not what platform or pulpit they speak from, nor what vast crowds they attract. Rather, do they care for the poor and needy members of God's family, Boaz-like, Jesus-like? Do they know that they themselves have been poor and needy and have received *hesed* from the Lord?[27]

This is Boaz. No wonder we are told in Ruth 2:1 that he is a worthy man, 'a man of standing' (NIV).

But notice that Boaz's loyalty-love, his faithfulness, are also manifested in the way in which he deals with matters that concern the heart.

A matter of the heart
Boaz has noticed more about Ruth than that she is a diligent worker. That emerges very clearly in chapter 3:10-11, and we need to steal a look at it now to grasp what is happening. Boaz comments there that Ruth has not 'gone after young men'. To say that, he must have noticed something about her. She is still physically attractive. Has he noticed the younger men looking in her direction? Is he saying, 'I see these young men; I see their

glances, and know what they are interested in; but I see how you respond'?

Boaz's affections and emotions have been touched. But it is his response to them that is so admirable. His reaction is marked by three things:

- respect: that is evident in all he says and does; he thinks first of Ruth;
- a desire to protect: he gives a particular warning to his men with respect to Ruth;[28]
- a willingness to provide.

These are the instincts that ought to govern any attraction to and affection for a woman in the heart of a man of God.

A marked contrast

But what does Boaz do at this point? He does his duty: he responds in grace and he acts with patience. Here Boaz seems to respond in marked contrast to the less spiritually stable and mature Naomi.

Notice how the narrative of chapter 2 ends. Ruth says, 'The man's name with whom I worked today is Boaz.' 'May he be blessed by the LORD,' Naomi says. But then she adds, 'The man is a close relative of ours, he is one of our redeemers.'

As the narrative flows on, it is almost as though Ruth has not noticed this, or perhaps not even understood it. She is too taken up with and overcome by the kindness of Boaz. It is Naomi who has begun to draw conclusions from circumstances. We can almost see the little wheels in her scheming mind: 'He is a relative; one of our "redeemers". This is our chance!' As we shall see in the next chapter, a *goel,* a 'redeemer', is exactly what these two women need. Boaz might just be the answer to all their problems. Naomi is already planning that he will be!

You can understand Naomi. After all these years away from the ordinances of God, you can see that her anxiety might well lead to impatience. You can understand if she now wants to take the answer to her prayers into her own hands and fulfil them in her own way. She and Elimelech did this before. You can understand why impatience might rear its ugly head again just at this crucial juncture.

But Boaz is patient. He is indeed a man of true substance, marked by duty, grace, patience, and covenant loyalty. Impressively, he is able to be this kind of man in a world in which he knows young men 'go after' young women, and young women 'go after' young men—our kind of world.

Character like this never appears on the spur of the moment, instantaneously. These are habits of the heart that have deep roots in our past, and are present as marks of general godliness before they ever come to expression in a specific crisis. As John Milton said so eloquently of Oliver Cromwell:

> *He was a soldier disciplined to perfection in the knowledge of himself. He had either extinguished, or by habit had learned to subdue, the whole host of vain hopes, fears, and passions, which infest the soul. He first acquired the government of himself, and over himself acquired the most signal victories, so that on the first day he took the field against the external enemy, he was a veteran in arms, consummately practised in the toils and exigencies of war.*[29]

So here stands this fine man and here is this younger woman, in both of whom God's *hesed* is bearing fruit in godly character. She, like him, is, in the profoundest sense, becoming a woman of substance, although her background is pagan idolatry.

They are well suited for one another. What will happen next?

Ruth 3: 1-18

*THEN Naomi her mother-in-law said to her, 'My daughter, should I not
seek rest for you, that it may be well with you? 2Is not Boaz our relative,
with whose young women you were? See, he is winnowing barley
tonight at the threshing floor. 3Wash therefore and anoint yourself, and
put on your cloak and go down to the threshing floor, but do not make
yourself known to the man until he has finished eating and drinking.
4But when he lies down, observe the place where he lies. Then go and
uncover his feet and lie down, and he will tell you what to do.' 5And she
replied, 'All that you say I will do.'*

*6So she went down to the threshing floor and did just as her mother-
in-law had commanded her. 7And when Boaz had eaten and drunk,
and his heart was merry, he went to lie down at the end of the heap
of grain. Then she came softly and uncovered his feet and lay down.
8At midnight the man was startled and turned over, and behold, a
woman lay at his feet! 9He said, 'Who are you?' And she answered, 'I
am Ruth, your servant. Spread your wings over your servant, for you
are a redeemer.' 10And he said, 'May you be blessed by the LORD, my
daughter. You have made this last kindness greater than the first in
that you have not gone after young men, whether poor or rich. 11And
now, my daughter, do not fear. I will do for you all that you ask, for all
my fellow townsmen know that you are a worthy woman. 12And now
it is true that I am a redeemer. Yet there is a redeemer nearer than I.
13Remain tonight, and in the morning, if he will redeem you,good; let
him do it. But if he is not willing to redeem you, then, as the LORD lives,
I will redeem you. Lie down until the morning.'*

*14So she lay at his feet until the morning, but arose before one could
recognize another. And he said, 'Let it not be known that the woman*

came to the threshing floor.' 15And he said, 'Bring the garment you
are wearing and hold it out.' So she held it, and he measured out six
measures of barley and put it on her. Then she went into the city. 16And
when she came to her mother-in-law, she said, 'How did you fare,
my daughter?' Then she told her all that the man had done for her,
17saying, 'These six measures of barley he gave to me, for he said to me,
"You must not go back empty-handed to your mother-in-law."' 18She
replied, 'Wait, my daughter,until you learn how the matter turns out,
for the man will not rest but will settle the matter today.'

Chapter Four
The midnight hour

'I remember your name in the night, O LORD, and keep your law.' (Psalm 119:55)

The book of Ruth has been aptly described as one of the greatest short stories ever written. But we have already discovered that it is not merely a story of human devotion and romance. Much more than that, it is a story about God's faithfulness, and a cameo portrait of two women into whose lives the great divine romance of God's lovingkindness and faithfulness has been painted.

Chapter 1 traces the wonder of God's providence in the way in which he brings people to trust in his covenant promise and grace. It is a narrative of a surprising conversion. Chapter 2 develops the storyline further, and in the process portrays the faithfulness that God's grace reproduces in his people. Godliness is God-likeness.

It may be commonplace to underline the importance of this—but it does need to be underlined: the only way most people we know will ever see the transforming grace of God is in our lives and characters. Ruth chapter 2 shows us how God's loyal love, his steadfastness, his grace, his desire to bring blessing at whatever expense to himself, are all reflected in Boaz and Ruth.

We have already hinted that it is probably intentional on the part of the author of Ruth that we should see the romantic dimension of his story as a replay of the first love-relationship in the Garden of Eden. God's grace restores what his love first created for us but sin has marred.

A distortion of grace?

Christians sometimes have a less than biblical view of grace. They see it as essentially antithetical to nature. Thus they conclude that the call of God involves a rejection of everything that is natural. This is sometimes reinforced by a misunderstanding of biblical expressions such as the 'natural' person and the 'spiritual' person,[30] or by a misconstruing of what Scripture means by 'the world'. But grace does not destroy nature—God's gifts in creation—it heals, restores and perfects it. The final goal of the work of Christ is the resurrection and transformation of the natural order that he brought into being at creation! Consequently, grace runs like a mountain stream into the river bed that sin has dried up. God makes the desert blossom like a rose!

Thus, in the sovereign purposes of God, Boaz and Ruth are 'meant' for one another. He has their natural human happiness in view (and, as we shall see, much more than their happiness!). In a fallen world there are obstacles in the way, road blocks that need to be dealt with. But we should never confuse those obstacles—real as they are— with the false idea that God is as likely to punish us as he is to bless us.

Obstacles

Biblical narratives often share a similar pattern: when the work of God begins to advance, obstacles appear in the way. As readers (or hearers) we find ourselves asking the question: In what way will God overcome these obstacles?

Our own lives as believers tell a similar story of obstacles to be faced and overcome. Sometimes these obstacles come from a world that is opposed to God. At other times it is we ourselves—believers—who act foolishly and as a result seem to endanger the plan of God. Think how often that was true in the life of Simon Peter. If he had had his way there would have been no cross for Jesus to carry—and no salvation for us! Many parts of Scripture tell the same story. We have an uncanny knack of marring God's good gifts and—if we were capable of it—endangering his gracious purposes.

Wise counsel?

Thus, chapter 3 of Ruth brings us to a disturbing element in the story. Here Naomi urges Ruth to make herself as attractive as possible,[31] go down to the threshing floor, and under cover of darkness 'uncover his [Boaz's] feet and lie down'. Naomi adds, 'and he will tell you what to do'.

Over the years both Jewish and Christian scholars have wondered whether these words should be translated with more obvious sexual undertones. But even as they read in our standard English translations this is hardly counsel we expect an older woman to give to an attractive young woman in her twenties. Can this be the same woman who has been restored by God's grace? Is she really telling her daughter-in-law to perfume herself, put on her most attractive clothes, go down to the threshing floor in the middle of the night, lie beside a man to whom she is not married, and wait to see what happens? Can this possibly be God's way of doing things? Is it conceivable that a sensible Christian would ever give counsel like this? Can it be divinely blessed? It may be, as some of the rabbis held, that the action would remind Boaz of his responsibility as a redeemer.[32] But if so, it is a foolhardy way to go about it!

These are the questions that come instinctively to mind, surely, as we read this passage. They can hardly be glossed over or sanitised by the notion that this was simply a traditional custom with nothing unusual about it at all. If we share this sense of anxiety, then the author of the book of Ruth has got us into precisely the frame of mind he wants to create! This is exactly what he intends us to feel. He wants us to feel our toes curling with anticipation: What is going on here? Is this story going to end in disaster?

We need to read on.

Redeemer

We have seen how the book of Ruth enhances our understanding of the purposes of God by throwing out an idea and then only later developing it.

Naomi's prayer that Ruth will experience the covenant loyalty of the Lord begins to be answered in the narrative of chapter 2. In addition, the narrator has given his readers a clue that is at the time hidden from Naomi and Ruth: the outstanding Boaz of Bethlehem is a relative of Elimelech. In chapter 2:20, when Ruth innocently mentions that she has been in the field of Boaz, Naomi responds not only with a benediction—'May he be blessed by the LORD'— but also adds, in what seems like a conspiratorial fashion, 'The man is a close relative of ours, one of our redeemers.'

To understand the narrative here, we need to have some knowledge of the role played by a redeemer.

The Mosaic law

When God called his people Israel into existence, he established them as his own family. The ordinances of his law made provision for their blessing even when they encountered distress and failure, difficulty and tragedy. Thus, among the institutions of the law was that of the family obligation to safeguard its members—particularly with respect to two central elements in the Abrahamic covenant: the continuation of the family and the enjoyment of the Promised Land.

If someone fell into need, a close family member was expected to volunteer to help—to become that person's redeemer (the noun for redeemer, *goel,* comes from the verb *galal:* 'to redeem' or 'deliver'). God describes himself as the Redeemer of his people (Exodus 6:6-8).[33] But God creates his people to be his image (Genesis 1:26-27). His covenant with them as their Redeemer when they were in bondage and need placed an obligation on them to redeem the needy.

Thus, in the case of loss of life by murder, a kinsman-redeemer would seek justice (Numbers 35:12). If a family member found himself in such debt that he sold himself into slavery, his kinsman-redeemer would pay to redeem him. If family property was mortgaged in one way or another, the kinsman-redeemer would regain it for the family (Leviticus 25:23-55). Underlying this was the fact that family members were God's servants, not any man's (v.55); and family land was God's land, given in trust (v.23). The blessing of God under the old covenant was integrally related to the land that God had parcelled out for his people. It was written into the law that the family land should remain within the family in perpetuity as a symbol of God's covenant blessing.

Family unity and covenant continuity

A similar principle of family unity and covenant continuity is found in Deuteronomy 25:5-10, in what is usually referred to as the *levirate* law. The word 'levirate' comes from the Latin word *levir*, which means a brother-in-law, although it is possible that the principle of levirate law extended beyond that relationship.

It seems clear from the exposition of the law by our Lord that the laws were specific illustrations of deep moral principles of life. The principle applied much more widely than the illustration. Thus, for example, according to Jesus, the commandment, 'You shall not commit adultery', includes lust (Matthew 5:27-30); 'You shall not murder' also forbids destroying someone's reputation with words (vv.21-26).

The principle underlying the levirate law was the importance of the continuity of the family line. Not only was life sacred, and the land sacred, but the continuity of God's covenant promises and their fulfilment from generation to generation was important. The levirate law stated that if a husband died childless, his brother (i.e. his widow's brother-in-law) would then father a son for the dead man.[34] By this means, the deceased man's name would not be forgotten and lost in Israel, and the promise of God—that he would bless a faithful man to generations yet unborn—would have visible, physical testimony among his people.

Pointing forwards

When we read the Old Testament, we always need to remember that God revealed himself in concrete, physical ways: in a land, in a family, in physical propagation and generation, in riches and poverty, in famine and plenty, and in the physical character of the liturgy and the sacrificial system. Before his final self-revelation in his Son made flesh (John 1:14), God was impressing lessons on his people by physical means. As Paul explains, the rituals of the Mosaic law acted like the slave who disciplined and guarded the son of a Roman father. They surrounded Israel (like an under-age child being taken to school) and pointed to the final sacrifice that was still to come. Thus, for example, the stench of blood in Jerusalem at the time when the Passover lambs were slaughtered must have been almost overpowering—tens and tens of thousands of animals were slain. The people were being pointed to the judgement their sins deserved, the substitute that God provided, and yet also to the fact that these animals could not take away the sins of human beings—only the Lamb of God, led to the slaughter, could do this (Isaiah 53:7). It was thus not possible to live under the old covenant without being confronted constantly by reminders of God's covenant provision and loyal love.

In the same way, the provision of a kinsman-redeemer pointed forwards to someone greater.

In the book of Ruth

Here the two women at the centre of our story are both widows. But they have something else in common. They have neither children nor land. It is, therefore, from one point of view, not surprising that Naomi's ears prick up when she hears that Ruth has been gleaning in the field of Boaz—a kinsman and therefore a potential redeemer!

The opening words of chapter 3 suggest that Naomi's mind goes into overdrive at this point! She turns to Ruth and says, 'My daughter, should I not seek rest for you, that it may be well with you? Is not Boaz our relative . . . ?' (cf. 2:20). There is ongoing debate about whether or not Naomi is thinking specifically here of levirate marriage, since Boaz is certainly not a brother-in-law. But the principles of God's laws were never limited merely to the strict letter and it is possible that this provision was interpreted and applied more broadly. Whether that is the case or not, certainly Naomi has marriage in mind!

It would be hard, then, to miss what Naomi is plotting! She is rapidly extrapolating from the providence of God to her own conclusions—not usually a wise procedure. Naomi remembers Boaz's *hesed* to Ruth and she puts two and two together: he is a redeemer, a potential saviour of the land; at the same time God 'just happened' to bring Boaz into the field where Ruth 'just happened' to be gleaning. A perfect match of law and providence, thinks Naomi!

Forcing the issue

So Naomi moves on to the next stage of her scheme. Why should she not give heaven a helping hand on earth? She gives Ruth her instructions:

> *See, he is winnowing barley tonight at the threshing floor. Wash therefore and anoint [i.e. perfume] yourself, and put on your cloak and go down to the threshing floor, but do not make yourself known to the man until he has finished eating and drinking. But when he lies down, observe the place where he lies. Then go and uncover his feet and lie down, and he will tell you what to do. (Ruth 3:3-4)*

This is, as we have seen, one of the passages in Ruth that has evoked a good deal of discussion. What are we to make of it? What will the kinsman-redeemer do? That is the question.

The author gives us a wonderful hint in the last words spoken by Naomi: 'He will tell you what to do.' Some of the other things Naomi has said seem very unwise. It is highly unlikely—although the story has at times been read this way—that this represents an ancient and widely recognised custom. But do these final words express a deep confidence in the moral and spiritual integrity of Boaz? Or do they suggest that even if moral compromise is involved, the end will justify the means, and Boaz's help will be secured, by fair means or foul? After all, there is no indication in the drama itself that Naomi has met Boaz. Indeed, intriguingly in a book that is two-thirds dialogue, while Naomi and Ruth, and Ruth and Boaz, engage in conversation at different points, Naomi and Boaz never do!

Happily, as we discover, Boaz can be trusted. He knows what to do—not because he is a redeemer (2:20), but because he has a godly character. Thus, while the story begins with these details of what Naomi plots and Ruth puts into effect, the real focus of the third chapter is on Boaz.

It is interesting to notice in passing the way this drama has developed The first chapter focuses on Naomi and what God is beginning to do through her in the life of Ruth. The second chapter brings together Ruth and Boaz as the spotlight shines upon the gracious characteristics that God has worked in them. Now the spotlight falls upon Boaz and his deep-seated godliness and piety. The story is going somewhere. We can guess the answer to the question Where? but we do not yet know How?

Watch, then, as the drama unfolds.

Exposed to risk

Tremendous risk is involved in this scheme in which Naomi and Ruth together participate—risk to Ruth particularly. But there are also serious questions, unsettling questions, about the risk to which Naomi is prepared to expose Boaz. Perfume, night-time, good food and wine, the warm physical closeness of an attractive woman . . . what man could miss the apparent message? Perhaps Boaz would be safe meeting Ruth in his field under the noonday sun when his workers casually (or perhaps enviously) gaze his way. But at the darkest hour of the night, with the sensuous aroma of a sweet perfume (perhaps she is wearing 'midnight'!), when physical attraction is awakened and opportunity near—would a man not find himself tempted, and is that not the central part of the plan?

Intriguingly, while Ruth follows Naomi's counsel, in the event she also adds words of her own: 'Spread your wings over your servant' (NIV: 'spread the corner of your garment over me'). She echoes the language that Boaz himself used when he spoke about Ruth coming to shelter under the wings of the Almighty (2:12), in a context where it has obvious reference to the covenant bond of marriage.[35]

It has been suggested—perhaps out of a sense of embarrassment as much as anything else—that Ruth's actions must be some kind of traditional act of proposal. Adescription of Ruth in the *Bethlehem Star* personal column would be unlikely to attract much interest: 'Single Moabite woman, widowed, childless, with mother-in-law, seeks well-to-do Bethlehem businessman with view to marriage; must love mother-in-law.' Is this the equivalent? That is scarcely a tenable view.

Nevertheless, there is more than one way to read Ruth's words. There is an ambiguity built into them—deliberately? Is Ruth simply saying to Boaz, 'Boaz, will you become the answer to your own prayer for my blessing?' or is there a hint of more—an invitation to physical, sexual intimacy? The tension of the story lies in the fact that the words are open to more than one interpretation. The word translated 'feet' ('uncover his feet', 3:4,7,8) is translated as 'legs' in Daniel 10:6. We are uncertain exactly what is happening here!

Behind her risky strategy lies Naomi's old spiritual rashness. It is the residue of the spirit that earlier led to emigration from the Promised Land. If God does not do things speedily enough for us in our way, then we will take matters into our own hands. We devise our own ways of bringing to pass what

God has promised to give to us. We refuse to wait for him to bring his own purposes to fruition.

Midnight darkness

It is characteristic of Old Testament narrative that all this should be expressed in an atmospheric way. That is always a mark of good storytelling; the emotion is sensed rather than stated. Here it is night-time. The night is the low point, the time of spiritual need and spiritual danger. At midnight the crisis comes.

The narrative began in daylight. But now it is dark. Indeed, this event could take place only in the darkness. It must be hidden, accomplished secretly and mysteriously. City dwellers, that is, most people in the western world, never really know what darkness is. You need to live miles away from large centres of population in order to experience true darkness—darkness in which you cannot see. In a really rural area you can put your hand up to your face but see nothing. That is the kind of darkness of rural Bethlehem in which Ruth is told to act. But it is in that deep darkness—the tension-packed danger point in this story—that Boaz's godliness shines. As he begins to speak, the light begins to dawn against the dark backcloth of Naomi's rash scheme.

There are other signs that Naomi is acting in a reckless manner. One is the way in which her counsel here seems contrary to her former moral concerns for Ruth. Earlier she said, 'It will be good for you, my daughter, to go with his girls because in someone else's field you might be harmed' (2:22 NIV). Harmed in the middle of the day? Yes—she is concerned for the preservation of her daughter-in-law, and that probably includes her sexual purity. But now she seems prepared to risk everything as she encourages her to go down to the threshing floor. We may assume that the threshing floor at harvest season was more dangerous morally at night-time than the open fields in daytime. Scripture later hints at this.[36] Indeed, we scarcely need it to tell us what we can already guess.

Secrecy is sometimes a sinister sign. 'Don't let him know you are there until he has finished eating and drinking. When he lies down . . . go and uncover his feet' (3:3-4 NIV). When you see a certain kind of secrecy—not a happy secrecy but a calculated one—in your children, you instinctively think, 'Something's up!' Why is it that they do not tell you? Because something is wrong. This also becomes clear from the words of Boaz (he recognises the danger, the compromising situation Naomi has engineered): 'Let it not be known that the woman came to the threshing floor' (v.14—to whom is he speaking?).

We must not totally misjudge Naomi. She has a sense of what God's providential purpose might be. But hunches about what God is doing should not be turned into schemes by which we engineer circumstances in order to bring those purposes to pass in an accelerated way. Naomi recognizes what God might be doing; but she does not submit herself to the principle that God's purposes are to be fulfilled in God's ways and at God's time.

By contrast, Boaz—in this context severely tried at Naomi's hands—is set before us as the model kinsman-redeemer. He is a man who, of course, desires the best for his own life under the providence of God, but who also has a resolute commitment to the principle that God's purposes must be fulfilled in God's ways and at God's time. Before Psalm 37 was written, Boaz illustrated its great maxim: 'Delight yourself in the LORD, and he will give you the desires of your heart' (v.4).

Lessons in guidance

This dramatic section of the narrative contains a great deal of practical instruction for us about the way in which we interpret the providences of God, and seek his guidance. It is worth pausing to reflect on some of these lessons as we see them modelled for us in Boaz.

What general lessons do we learn from Boaz about how to interpret the providences of God?

- Boaz has developed a commitment never to run ahead of God.
- Boaz understands that the providences of God in our lives are not, in and of themselves, self-interpreting. They must always be interpreted in the light of the teaching given to us in God's Torah, his trustworthy word. Scripture (in Boaz's case this is limited to the Pentateuch) provides the lenses through which we interpret and respond to every providence of God.
- Boaz recognises that love for a woman implies responsibilities towards her family. While marriage involves a new family unit (a man 'leaves' his parents in order to 'hold fast' to his wife, Genesis 2:24), he does not abandon either his or his new wife's family. 'Love me, love my family' is part and parcel of marriage—even when families are difficult! In this case, Boaz is implicitly being asked to love and care for Ruth's mother-in-law—her *first* husband's mother—a challenging calling!

Boaz is an outstanding example of a biblically instructed man who makes wise instinctive responses in a critical situation. He knows how to apply the principles of godliness found in Scripture. He thinks biblically. He well illustrates the principle of John Newton that we learn to recognise the guidance of God in our lives 'as a musical ear judges of sounds'[37]—by developing biblical instincts. We do not carry around a Bible concordance. Rather, we hide the word of God in our hearts (Psalm 119:11). Its implications and applications flow naturally into our lives as we find ourselves in a variety of circumstances. God has not left us to interpret providence on our own. Boaz has learned the important lesson that 'Providence is a Christian's diary, not his Bible!'[38]

A time to embrace?

Boaz's example also points us to principles specifically helpful when we are engaged in courtship and contemplating marriage. We have already noticed that this whole section of Ruth is a kind of re-run of Eden. It shows how in a fallen world God brings together a man and a woman in trust, devotion and love, for lifelong friendship, for mutual help and encouragement, and for family life.

Boaz seems to have a clearer idea of and trust in God's ways than Naomi does; for all that her anxiety is understandable; in her circumstances most of us would share her panic. Naomi is an engineer of romance. She issues a whole series of excited commands to her daughter-in-law: 'This is what you have to do.' But there is a kind of feverishness about her desire for 'God's will' to be done— a trait by no means exclusive to women, or to the area of romance! It suggests that she is not sufficiently distinguishing the purposes of the divine will from the desires of the human heart. Restlessness of this kind must always be watched carefully.

By contrast, the response of Boaz—not because he is a man, but because he is consistently godly—is characterized by a deep-seated trust that God is well able to bring his purposes to pass in his own ways and in his own time. And that includes the meeting of his deep and instinctive desire for a life companion.

Caveats

Having noticed these points, however, there are also some things that should be said to avoid misunderstanding.

Recognising the un-wisdom of Naomi's counsel should not lead us to issue a trumpet blast against perfume or attractive clothing! Beauty and attractiveness are not the same thing as seduction. Christians are not called to a life of dowdiness.[39] In fact, Scripture makes much of attractiveness, counselling us only to match outer attractiveness with inner grace. Our covenant Lord has 'made everything beautiful in its time' (Ecclesiastes 3:11).

There is a beauty that is only skin-deep. And the skin fades. It is shrewd enough advice to give young men and women on the verge of developing a close relationship: 'Take a look at her mother or his father: that is what she or he may look like in thirty years' time!'We need to be confident that the physical attractiveness we see now is blended with a character that is growing in inward beauty, and that this is a companion we will love when youthful looks fade. Marriage is for life! Will lasting beauty sustain lasting attraction?

There is another principle here. It is possible for us, in our fear of missing the will of God, to become paralysed. But here our hero Boaz, in his response to Ruth, is not only careful to express the wisdom of God's word but also to give expression to the God-given affection, appreciation and admiration that he feels for Ruth. In addition, because he is absolutely committed to God's ways, he will do nothing to compromise either his or Ruth's integrity. He is committed to the principle that he will not say or do anything that might endanger a burgeoning friendship that, at the end of the day, may not lead to marriage.

But we need to express this positively. Boaz rejoices in Ruth because of who and what she is, and because of the fruits of

God's providence and grace in her. We feel sure by this point that this story will end in either great happiness or poignant sadness. We expect it will be happiness, for this narrative has a kind of 'all's well that ends well' feel about it.

An echo

So we are right to hear in Boaz an echo of Adam rejoicing at his first sight of Eve. Boaz as much as says to Ruth: 'You are exactly what I have been looking for; I am thrilled to have found you.' He recognises in her a soul-mate; his *hesed* is matched by her *hesed*. But he is sensitive to the wisdom that would later find expression in the experience of the Preacher: 'Better one hand full with quietness than both the hands full with travail and vexation of spirit' (Ecclesiastes 4:6).

The language used by Adam in the Genesis account of creation helps us to understand what is involved here. His instinctive response to his first sight of Eve was to recognize that she was someone different from him (she was another person and a woman!). Yet she was someone in whom he could see himself—in distinction from all the other life forms in creation she was 'fit for' or 'corresponding to' him (Genesis 2:18-20). In this sense, Eve was the one companion fully suited to him, who would turn the 'not good' of his being alone into the 'very good' of a new, covenant relationship in which he would discover at a new depth what it meant to be the image of God, sharing now—as his triune Creator had done from all eternity— in a world of intimate fellowship with another who shared his nature.

Boaz similarly hopes that God is giving him someone spiritually compatible with himself, and at the same time physically suited to him and his graces as well as his needs.

An excellent woman

All this is brought out in a beautifully subtle way: Boaz uses language about Ruth that the narrator has earlier used about Boaz!

Boaz, we are told, is 'a worthy man' [2:1; NIV: 'a man of standing']'. We have discovered that he is a man of substance in every sense—character as well as riches. And now he knows that the word on the street about Ruth is true: she is 'a worthy woman' (3:11), a woman of genuine spiritual substance. The same expression reappears in the wonderful poem in praise of 'an excellent wife' in Proverbs 31:10-31. Boaz is saying: 'I value what your friendship and love might mean to me more than I value anything else. Can it be that in you I am discovering the Lord's purpose for me?' Yet he is also saying to God: 'I want to submit my natural instincts and my desires for myself to whatever is your will for my life; for that alone is best for me. And the way in which I am going to do that is by fulfilling my biblical duties in this providential situation, and trusting that you will lead me into the future.'

Christians in an earlier generation rarely thought of writing books on guidance. There is a reason for that (just as there is a reason why so many of us today are drawn to books that will tell us how to find God's will). Our forefathers in the faith were catechised, and they taught catechisms to their children. Often as much as half of the catechism would be devoted to an exposition of the answers to questions like the following:

> *Question: Where do we find God's will?*
> *Answer: In the Scriptures.*
> *Question: Where in particular in the Scriptures?*
> *Answer: In the Commandments that God has given to us.*

Why were these questions and answers so important? Because these Christians understood that God's law provides basic guidelines that cover the whole of life. Indeed, in the vast majority of instances, the answer to the question 'What does

God want me to do?' will be found by answering the question: 'How does the law of God apply to this situation? What does the Lord require of me here in his Word?'

That is what characterises Boaz. He submits himself to working out the principles of God's law in order that he might allow God's purposes to be fulfilled in God's time. He well illustrates Jesus' teaching: 'Whoever has my commandments and keeps them, he it is who loves me' (John 14:21). Practical obedience is the fruit of love, not an expression of legalism.

Exposed to rashness

There is a further feature of this whole incident in which Boaz is exposed to the rashness of Naomi's plans.

Think of the situation. You have been threshing your grain. It is now late at night; you are tired but have enjoyed the food and wine of your evening meal. You lie down under the stars; the Lord is blessing your life. Suddenly you are startled out of your sleep. There is a movement at your feet. Someone is there.

There may even be an element of comic relief to lighten the tension here. The situation is graphically described in the text: Boaz shudders in the middle of the night and wakes up—just as we sometimes do when we discover that the bed cover, or duvet, has fallen on the floor. Boaz has a sense that someone else is there; almost simultaneously he becomes aware of the scent of perfume lingering in the air. It is a woman, and a woman who has deliberately made herself attractive. The atmosphere is full of danger.

How does Boaz respond to what seems such a threateningly compromising situation?[40]

Poise

First, Boaz responds with remarkable poise. What are you like when you wake up in the middle of the night? That is partly a matter of personal disposition. Some people should never be disturbed at breakfast time, never mind in the middle of the night! Families understand that everybody gets out of bed in a different mood: some are immediately full of energy; for others the last thing in the world they want is for anybody to speak to them.

Boaz shudders. It is cold. Or it may be simply that he is startled into consciousness. How will he respond in a crisis? And how would you respond?

Once, at the end of a meal in a Chinese restaurant in Philadelphia, my daughter opened her 'fortune cookie'. Sometimes the little slips of paper inside these cookies promise future happiness; sometimes they give proverbial counsel. Hers read: *Never mistake temptation for opportunity.* Wise words indeed.

Boaz could easily have made that mistake. He was a redblooded and sinful man. He could easily have taken advantage of the situation and excused himself by the rashness of Naomi and the naïveté of Ruth. But the impressive thing is that when Boaz wakens in the middle of the night—even before he has time to think carefully—God and his ways are in the centre of his thoughts! God has so worked grace into his life that in this crisis moment he remains calm, a man of poise. However much he may naturally be astonished, his basic equilibrium is not unsettled. He thinks— and thinks biblically. That is a hallmark of faith.

Recall the apostle Paul in the Mediterranean storm, taking charge of a situation in which military men panic;[41] or the Lord Jesus, similarly endangered on the Sea of Galilee, sleeping while hardened fisherman cry out in fear;[42] or Simon Peter, in prison, anticipating possible execution, sleeping when God sends an angel to rescue him.[43] What is it that is characteristic of them all? God's grace enabled them to maintain their equilibrium; their hearts and minds were guarded in the peace and love of God.[44]

Such poise is not in us by nature. It comes from meditation on God's Word, a life transformed by a renewed mind, uncompromised commitment to pleasing him, and an assurance that his ways are best (Romans 12:1-2). Only a life embedded in the sovereign grace of God, the fruit of a heart that has been meditating upon his Word, enables us to bear this rich fruit of grace.

So Boaz shows remarkable poise. But coupled with it is absolute integrity.

Integrity

As a teenager, Jonathan Edwards, the eighteenth-century theologian and philosopher, wrote a series of personal resolutions. One was this:

> *Resolved: Never to do any manner of thing whether in soul or body, less or more, but what tends to the glory of God . . .*[45]

Similar commitment has made Boaz 'a worthy man' (2:1). It is the key to his character. He sees what he should do not simply by asking the question, 'What am I to do?' but by asking, 'How may I best glorify God?'

Having already spoken in a kindly way to Ruth (2:13), he now does so again. He is concerned for her public reputation—

no matter what happens between them. For she is in serious spiritual and moral danger at the threshing floor. The thing Boaz is most concerned about is not simply his own integrity, but preserving her integrity, and protecting her in her time of need. In that sense Boaz, our hero, is like the great Hero; he is so Christlike.

It would be a mistake to think of Boaz as a 'type' of Christ in the technical sense. But there is a sense in which Old Testament believers belong to Christ and, like New Testament believers, have their lives shaped into the likeness of Christ (Romans 8:29). Their lives act like intimations of Christ's coming and character. So here. Boaz exemplifies the grace that our Lord demonstrated when he faced the greatest crisis of his life and ministry. He, too, was concerned for the preservation and the protection of those he loved. He spoke with deep kindness of heart to his disciples, and prayed for them.[46]

Boaz expresses a gracious respect for Ruth:

> *May you be blessed by the LORD, my daughter. You have made this last kindness greater than the first in that you have not gone after young men, whether poor or rich.*[47] *And now, my daughter, do not fear. I will do for you all that you ask . . . you are a worthy woman.* (3:10-11)

He is very gentle with this new believer. He does not manhandle her, and brush her aside with incriminating or derogatory words—'Get out of here! Don't you have any idea what it means to live a covenant life? How dare you do this?' Think of how that would have crushed Ruth's already bruised spirit. It might well have destroyed her. But instead Boaz speaks with a tenderness and graciousness that marks him out as precisely the kind of man this young woman really needs.

Alexander Whyte, the famous nineteenth-century Scottish minister, used to say, 'There is such a thing as sanctification by vinegar'—an acidic correctness that leaves a sharp and unpleasant taste in the mouth. Vinegar may enhance the flavour of food, but it is not itself nourishing.

As youngsters we used to play conkers in the horse-chestnut season. A conker was a chestnut through the core of which a piece of string was threaded. The players took alternate swipes at each other's conker until one or other broke in pieces. Like scalps, a conker was known by the number of wins it had amassed! We all knew how to cheat (even if we did not personally succumb to the temptation!). You soaked your conker overnight in vinegar to harden it so that it would splinter the softer shell of an opponent's nut.

Sadly, there are hard-shell Christians who exude a kind of metallic, unyielding, 'correct' spirit. In the end, that is an un-Christlike character. Nobody in need wants to pour their heart out to a person sanctified by vinegar. By contrast, real sanctification is becoming more like Jesus—truly, fully, attractively human. It is produced not by 'correctness' but by grace—Boaz-like, Jesus-like grace.

Personal disposition

Those who knew Boaz even a little would know that his covenant God must be a God of tenderness and compassion, of great sweetness and gentleness in his righteous dealings with his children. We cannot hide what we really believe God is like. Our personal disposition is an unending expression of our understanding of and trust in his character. How we live, how we respond to challenges, crises and trials, reveals what we really believe about God, what we really think 'deep down' about him.

The strange Danish genius Søren Kierkegaard noted this in a penetrating entry in his Journal in 1850. He was commenting on the significance of home and family life with respect to the development of faith in children. Most commentators assume that the insight he recorded reflects his own home:

> *The greatest danger for a child, where religion is concerned*
>
> *The greatest danger is not that his father or tutor should be a free-thinker, not even his being a hypocrite. No, the danger lies in his being a pious, God-fearing man, and in the child being convinced thereof, but that he should nevertheless notice that deep in his soul there lies hidden an unrest which, consequently, not even the fear of God and piety could calm. The danger is that the child in this situation is almost provoked to draw a conclusion about God, that God is not infinite love.*[48]

That principle is widely applicable. When it comes to their sense of the character of the One in whom we profess to trust, others 'breathe in' what we 'breathe out'. It is because he trusts his God that Boaz is content to apply biblical principles to his situation, to do his duty, and to leave the consequences to the wise and good providence of God.

Calming a troubled mind

Boaz has been subjected to rash treatment at the hands of Naomi. But he has displayed amazing poise in the crisis of the night. Now this third act of the drama ends on an upbeat note that is also expressed atmospherically. It is calculated to make us smile. Boaz brings a deep assurance to these women, and perhaps especially to the over-anxious Naomi!

Boaz is like that. He imitates the character of the God who comes to his people with armloads of grace and mercy (Psalm

130:7). His first concern is for the protection of the young Ruth; then he wants to provide for her and her mother-in-law Naomi. He is the epitome of the later words of Micah:

He has told you, O man, what is good;
and what does the LORD require of you
but to do justice, and to love kindness [hesed],
and to walk humbly with your God?
(Micah 6:8)

Notice how the refrain that runs through the book like a melody line surfaces once again:

Naomi went out full and came back empty.
Now Ruth has gone out empty but is coming back full.

This was true already in chapter 2. Here it is even more emphatic. Boaz protects both his own and Ruth's reputation: 'Let it not be known that the woman came to the threshing floor.' But he does more, as his words indicate: 'Bring the garment you are wearing and hold it out' (3:15; Ruth, it seems, has a shawl around her, presumably to keep her warm, and perhaps also to cover up her identity). Into that shawl in which her empty life has been hidden, Boaz pours grain—six measures of barley!

Some commentators are at a loss to interpret this because it seems to be an overwhelming amount of barley. Yet the amount is deliberately emphasised. Perhaps there is again a moment of quiet humour here as Ruth looks at the amount of grain in the dawning light. Are we to imagine a look on her face that says: 'You're not going to tell me to carry that home, are you?' Perhaps we are meant to be spectators of this awkward, humorous, but engagingly ordinary moment in this burgeoning romance as Boaz says, 'Bend over', gathers the grain in the shawl and gently eases it on to Ruth's shoulders, or perhaps her head and shoulders? Is there a smile playing on Boaz's lips as he says, 'Take this home to that mother-in-law of yours. Make sure you tell her, "Boaz gave me these six measures of barley and told me to tell you he didn't want me to go back to my mother-in-law empty-handed."'

Boaz is sending a signal to Naomi that he understands. He is saying, 'I understand the need and I understand the panic. I understand why you did this. I don't approve. But my heart is open to you in grace, and this is a little message to you. Trust in the provision that God will supply.'

This is certainly not what either woman expected. But Boaz displays *hesed.* This action demonstrates the patience and kindness that is characteristic of God and also of his servants. He does not break a bruised reed or quench a dimly burning wick (Isaiah 42:3). How like Jesus![49] There may well be more than meets the eye in the fact that one of the two great bronze pillars at the vestibule to Solomon's temple was named 'Boaz'.[50] Indeed, when we discover where the book of Ruth fits in to the overall divine strategy, we will discover that in the building of God's ultimate temple, Boaz is a more significant figure than we could ever have imagined.[51]

Try to imagine the scene as Ruth returns. She is coming home as the new day dawns. Does Naomi see the burden Ruth is carrying? Naomi's deepest thoughts are anxious ones, for she surely understands the high-risk strategy she has adopted. For all the appearance of being casual, together, in control, she is longing to ask, 'How did things go?' Inwardly she is torn by anxiety and fear. Perhaps she has been up all night worrying—a nervous wreck!

So Ruth returns, the faintly unpleasant odour of perspiration replacing that of the earlier perfume. Naomi hears her coming and perhaps adopts an outwardly calm expression that masks her inner forebodings. Ruth is now perhaps almost collapsing under the weight of grain she is bringing home! 'How did it go, my daughter? What has happened?' (3:16). Are we meant to see Ruth turning to her, gasping, 'Boaz said—do not—go back—to your mother-in-law— empty-handed'?

As the grain in Ruth's shawl spills over on to the floor, does Naomi get the message, at last? She returned from Moab 'empty' (1:21). She will be empty no longer!

From plot to plenty

The beginning and the end of this scene stand in marked contrast. When it opens, Naomi is plotting and scheming: 'My daughter, should not I try to find a home for you where you will be well provided for? Boaz! Isn't he the man? He is a kinsman. Tonight he will be at the winnowing floor. Wash yourself. Perfume yourself. Disguise yourself . . .' Detail by detail she works out her plan. A mother-in-law like that might drive many of us to distraction!

But notice what Naomi says *now.* As though this sack (or shawl) of grain has become a sacrament of God's gracious purposes to her, she says to Ruth: Wait, trust. 'Wait, my daughter, until you find out what happens. For the man will not rest until the matter is settled today' (3:18 NIV).

The purpose of God

At the end of the day, the book of Ruth must be interpreted within a series of concentric contexts. It is the story of God's *hesed* to these two women. Of that *hesed* Boaz is the mediator. But it will eventually become clear that God's *hesed* stretches beyond these women to his greater purposes to establish the throne of David. In that purpose Boaz plays an essential role.

But beyond even this lies God's ultimate purpose in the coming of Christ and the establishing of his kingdom. We see a pattern in Boaz that points to the grace of which Christ would be the embodiment and final mediator. In this re-run of Eden's broken romance, but now in a fallen world, Boaz's bride will come to him, not fresh from the hands of God but through the sovereign activity of God in his kind and overruling providence. But like Adam with Eve, Boaz welcomes Ruth, protects and preserves her, so that they may walk in God's ways.

More than that, here in a fallen world this new man saves the woman and provides for her needs so that they may live in a pure communion. If anyone in Bethlehem wanted to explain to a stranger how Yahweh has loved his people in the covenant in which he betrothed Israel to himself, all they would need to do would be to say four words: 'As Boaz loves Ruth.'

Boaz's love, his *hesed* towards Ruth, shows us why God chose the love that leads to marriage as the great illustration of his relationship with his people—as will become clear in the New Testament.[52] Boaz is a true man, a reminder of what the first Adam was by creation and what the last Adam will be in re-creation.

This, then, is a little hint of the way in which God will ultimately bring salvation to his people; not in Adam, or in Boaz the kinsman-redeemer, but in Jesus Christ, the great kinsman-redeemer of whom his Father could say: Wait, because this Man will not rest until it is finished.

As Martin Luther memorably expressed it:

Did we in our own strength confide,
Our striving would be losing;
Were not the right Man on our side,
The Man of God's own choosing.

Dost ask who that may be?
Christ Jesus, it is he;
Lord Sabaoth his name,
From age to age the same,
And he must win the battle.[53]

We know even better than Boaz, and certainly better than Naomi did, that because God made his own Son our kinsman-redeemer,[54] not sparing him the cost of saving us, we can be confident that he will freely give us everything we shall ever need (Romans 8:32). Thus we learn to trust him.

God's timing

Shortly after Elijah's spiritual exertions on Mount Carmel, when he had been such a mighty and apparently fearless instrument of God's purposes, he began to feel that everything was falling apart in his hands. The desires of his heart were not being met by his God—so he felt. But God is never absent. The mood is wonderfully captured by Felix Mendelssohn in his great oratorio, *Elijah*. He portrays the prophet, following his lamentation, 'My labour is in vain', hearing the voice of an angel singing the marvellous words from the psalter: 'O rest in the Lord, wait patiently for him, and he will give thee thy heart's desires' (cf. Psalm 37:4,7).

In her desire to see her own and Ruth's needs met, Naomi acted rashly. It is easy to be like her. We are often in a greater hurry than God is. We need to learn that our God is trustworthy, his timing is perfect, his wisdom plans everything for our good. We have every reason to rest in the Lord and wait patiently for him.

There is never a good reason to run ahead of God.

Ruth 4: 1-22

*NOW Boaz had gone up to the gate and sat down there. And behold,
the redeemer, of whom Boaz had spoken, came by. So Boaz said, 'Turn
aside, friend; sit down here.' And he turned aside and sat down. 2And he
took ten men of the elders of the city and said, 'Sit down here.' So they
sat down. 3Then he said to the redeemer, 'Naomi, who has come back
from the country of Moab, is selling the parcel of land that belonged to
our relative Elimelech. 4So I thought I would tell you of it and say, "Buy
it in the presence of those sitting here and in the presence of the elders
of my people." If you will redeem it, redeem it. But if you will not, tell
me, that I may know, for there is no one besides you to redeem it, and I
come after you.' And he said, 'I will redeem it.' 5Then Boaz said, 'The day
you buy the field from the hand of Naomi, you also acquire Ruth the
Moabite, the widow of the dead, in order to perpetuate the name of the
dead in his inheritance.' 6Then the redeemer said, 'I cannot redeem it for
myself, lest I impair my own inheritance. Take my right of redemption
yourself, for I cannot redeem it.'*

*7Now this was the custom in former times in Israel concerning
redeeming and exchanging: to confirm a transaction, the one drew off
his sandal and gave it to the other, and this was the manner of attesting
in Israel. 8So when the redeemer said to Boaz, 'Buy it for yourself,' he
drew off his sandal. 9Then Boaz said to the elders and all the people,
'You are witnesses this day that I have bought from the hand of Naomi
all that belonged to Elimelech and all that belonged to Chilion and to
Mahlon. 10Also Ruth the Moabite, the widow of Mahlon, I have bought
to be my wife, to perpetuate the name of the dead in his inheritance,
that the name of the dead may not be cut off from among his brothers
and from the gate of his native place. You are witnesses this day.'
11Then all the people who were at the gate and the elders said, 'We are*

*witnesses. May the LORD make the woman, who is coming into your
house, like Rachel and Leah, who together built up the house of Israel.
May you act worthily in Ephrathah and be renowned in Bethlehem,
12and may your house be like the house of Perez, whom Tamar bore
to Judah, because of the offspring that the LORD will give you by this
young woman.'*

*13So Boaz took Ruth, and she became his wife. And he went in to her,
and the LORD gave her conception, and she bore a son. 14Then the
women said to Naomi, 'Blessed be the LORD, who has not left you this
day without a redeemer, and may his name be renowned in Israel! 15He
shall be to you a restorer of life and a nourisher of your old age, for your
daughter-in-law who loves you, who is more to you than seven sons,
has given birth to him.' 16Then Naomi took the child and laid him on
her lap and became his nurse. 17And the women of the neighbourhood
gave him a name, saying, 'A son has been born to Naomi.' They named
him Obed. He was the father of Jesse, the father of David.*

*18Now these are the generations of Perez: Perez fathered Hezron,
19Hezron fathered Ram, Ram fathered Amminadab, 20Amminadab
fathered Nahshon, Nahshon fathered Salmon, 21Salmon fathered
Boaz, Boaz fathered Obed, 22Obed fathered Jesse, and Jesse fathered
David.*

Chapter Five
Mission accomplished

'And we know that for those who love God all things work together for good, for those who are called according to his purpose.' (Romans 8:28)

The fourth chapter of Ruth is not only the last chapter in the book, it is also the climax. Here the purposes of God—or at least the next stage in his purposes—begin to become clear.

At the personal level, the message of the book of Ruth is of God's faithful love, leading to restoration and blessing— both physical and spiritual. We have already noted the subtle way in which the author hints at this throughout the opening chapter, by his use, on a dozen or so occasions, of the Old Testament verb *shub,* the Hebrew verb for 'returning', 'turning back', 'restoring', 'repenting'. What God does in the lives of these two women then becomes a hint of what he will do on a broader scale. He brings restoration where there has been sin and rebellion.

In that sense, this book is a cameo portrait of the gospel and of the grace of God. God, as Jeremiah realised, is a potter; he can destroy what is marred by sin. But he can also remake what has been spoiled.[55] He works all things (yes, all things) together for the good of those who love him, whatever their sins may be. He brings his purpose to fruition. As we explore the *hesed* of God in this Old Testament book, this is precisely what we have seen: God working everything together for good in a fallen world, for those who love him, however faintly and sometimes waywardly. In the original creation, God did not need to 'work' everything together for good. He simply spoke everything into existence, and it was very good. But in a fallen world God must do more than speak. It is as though God has to roll his sleeves up and work his good purposes into the material of a fallen creation against its innate tendency. His ultimate purpose is to magnify his glory; the central means by which he will do it is by creating in his people nothing less than the image of his Son in order that he might be the firstborn of a whole family that shares a family likeness to the elder brother (Romans 8:29).

Multi-tasking God

We must never limit the purposes of God, as though he were doing only one thing at a time in only one person and one place at a time—here and now in me! Sometimes we can be deeply puzzled by the circumstances of our lives: what is God doing? Too frequently we focus attention on ourselves as though the answer lay within our individual lives—as if we were the central key to interpreting the plan of the God of the entire universe!

God is intimately aware of us and deeply concerned for our welfare. But his providential purposes, which *include* me, do not *centre* on me, as though what he is doing in me could be isolated from everything else he is doing! No, God's purposes criss-cross and zigzag, and cross-fertilise one believer's life with that of an unbeliever, or one believer's experience with another believer. He is always simultaneously and contemporaneously doing several things in several lives.

We see that principle at work in Naomi's little family circle, as though we were looking through a microscope. There is a marvel and beauty to the divine mosaic of providence, although it is often beyond the powers of the naked eye to see until we wear biblically-crafted lenses in the spectacles through which we see and interpret life. We need to learn to walk not by our natural sight but by faith-sight, if we are to discern what Paul calls God's 'multicoloured wisdom' (Ephesians 3:10). It is, as we have seen, marvellously displayed here.

The final obstacle

We have seen how Naomi very nearly became a serious obstacle to the ongoing purposes of God. And yet through her actions God's purposes were nevertheless being advanced. Now we will witness the removal of a final obstacle to his blessing in the lives of these three people. At the threshing floor, Boaz said to Ruth:

> *May you be blessed by the LORD, my daughter. You have made this last kindness greater than the first in that you have not gone after young men, whether poor or rich. And now, my daughter, do not fear. I will do for you all that you ask . . . it is true that I am a redeemer. Yet there is a redeemer nearer than I. (Ruth 3:10-12)*

We can imagine Naomi hearing from her perspiring daughter the news of everything that Boaz has said, and then thinking, 'Why does there always have to be a snag? Why do God's people have to be marked by such integrity?' Boaz says there is an obstacle. While his heart is Ruth's and it is his deep desire to marry her, there is something more important to him: his heart is the Lord's before it is hers.

Some words written by Temple Gairdner of Cairo a century ago express Boaz's spirit. On the eve of his wedding, he penned these lines:

> *That I may come near to her, draw me nearer to Thee than to her;*
> *that I may know her, make me to know Thee more than her;*
> *that I may love her with the perfect love of a perfectly whole heart,*

cause me to love Thee more than her and most of all.
Amen. Amen.[56]

Nor was this the impulse of the moment. Significantly, Gairdner had earlier written in his journal:

> *Prayed definitely that I may be a man and have a heart one day pure and noble enough to be owned by and to own a woman's heart.*[57]

But will God solve the problem of a nearer redeemer, the relative on whom the responsibility to help these women falls before it falls on Boaz? This is the storyline in the final chapter. If and when God does this, the message of the book of Ruth will draw to a conclusion—or so we think!

A theological symphony

The structure of the entire book merits comment here. There is a beauty to it that matches the story it tells. It begins with a description of Naomi and the three men who surround her, Elimelech, Mahlon and Chilion. Each man has died and has no actual part in the narrative of the story. Naomi, Ruth and Boaz step on to centre stage. Fascinatingly, the book ends with the reversal of that order: first Boaz, then Ruth, and finally Naomi, disappear from sight.

This gives us a satisfying sense of completeness and orderliness, of God restoring the fractured disorder of life, putting the finishing touches to his work, and bringing his purposes to completion to his own satisfaction. This is what the Bible means by the peace or *shalom* of God. It underlines the ultimate orderliness of God's ways. The whole atmosphere of the closing chapter is meant to convey to us a sense that he does all things well.

At the end of the chapter, we are given a list of people who have not yet lived but who will be profoundly influenced by the events that have just been described. Now we learn that the deeper significance of what God is doing lies well beyond the lifetime of its central characters. The book of Ruth is a theological symphony, but one that long lay unfinished. The words of Naomi speak truth that go far beyond her wildest imagination. While her native tendency is to demand hurried divine activity to fit her plans, the last recorded words she speaks in the book are: 'Wait, my daughter . . . for [God's] man will not rest but will settle the matter today' (3:18). Wait!

It takes faith to learn this lesson, and—in Shakespeare's words—to discover:

> *There's a divinity that shapes our ends,*
> *Rough-hew them how we will.*[58]

The metaphor here is derived from the cutting of English country hedgerows. Two men would work together on the hedge—one cutting vigorously, the other doing the detailed work of shaping. So it is with Naomi. She has been roughhewing in a major way. But God has shaped his own design. He can be trusted. He knew what was best all along. And he has a far greater purpose than Naomi can understand—why, therefore, does she fret? Now she is beginning to see that God's big purposes take time!

One of the lessons we learn from seeing the book of Ruth in the context of the whole Bible is that there are interim as well as final consummations to God's purposes. We look for the coming of our Lord Jesus Christ and for the consummation of the purposes of God. But, wonderfully, he keeps on giving us foretastes of the final consummation by the way in which he brings his plans for us to interim points of completion on the small scale of our present experience. The fact that he is able to work thus on the small scale of our apparently insignificant lives, encourages us to believe that he is also working out a larger master plan for the world. And he always puts the finishing touches to the work he begins (Philippians 1:6). So here he completes the good work that he has begun in Boaz, and then in Ruth, and finally, in Naomi.

Blessings for Boaz

In the first half of Ruth 4, we are made aware of the blessings that the Lord has brought to Boaz. Of course, Ruth and Naomi have very obvious needs. It might be tempting to see Boaz in marked contrast to them. But he, too, has needs. Boaz, like Adam, appears first on the scene as 'a worthy man' ('a man of standing', NIV). Adam was the master of the entire animal kingdom; he was the guardian of a marvellous garden, the steward of God's world, made for intimate friendship with his Master and Lord. Yet there was one thing about his life that was 'not good' (Genesis 2:18). He was alone. So, too, Boaz. Like Adam, he was not made to be alone.

Then, in echoes of Genesis 2, just as God gave to Adam a woman who was suited to him, creating her out of Adam's side, so God gave Ruth to Boaz. Does the author of Ruth find a certain pleasure in noting that Boaz awakes out of sleep—like Adam—to find at his side the woman whom God has brought to him (in this instance from Moab rather than from his rib cage)? Not out of Boaz's physical side but out of God's providential grace God has fitted them for each other.

This is a more dramatic replay of the first marriage than even the wonderful story of father Abraham's search for a wife for his son Isaac. Abraham's servant has been sent to seek a bride in a 'far country'. But here God himself goes to the 'far country' of Moab to bring back a bride for his son Boaz. What lengths God will go to! That is exactly the point! It will finally be made in the coming of Christ into the 'far country' for his bride the church:

From heaven he came and sought her
To be his holy bride;
With his own blood he bought her
And for her life he died.[59]

But when we focus more narrowly upon this narrative, it answers a more specific question: not, 'Does God bless his people according to his purpose?' but, 'By what means does God bring blessing to his people?' This story tells us of one means.

At the city gate

Boaz is determined to settle the matter. He rises early in the morning, goes out to the city gate, and waits for the town fathers (who acted as counsellors and judges). We can well imagine he is more than a little nervous. What will happen? Then, just as he is sitting there at the gate, 'behold' (the author's way of raising his eyebrow at us as if to say, 'There goes God's providential activity again!'), the closer relative whom Boaz has mentioned to Ruth just 'happens' to appear.

Boaz says to the relative: 'Turn aside, friend, sit down here' (NIV: ' . . . over here, my friend'). But the term translated 'friend' should not be understood as a sign of long intimacy. The word in Hebrew means something more like 'so and so'—as if Boaz has said: 'Over here, buddy boy', or even, 'Hey, pal, come over here'!

The anonymity of the relative (Boaz, after all, certainly knows his name!) adds an atmospheric touch to the drama. It serves to underline that this man will have no role in the advance of God's kingdom; he refuses to fulfil his covenant obligations. It is as though the narrator is saying, 'Do you see this man who refuses responsibility? He will have no further significance. He will remain unnamed, and have no place in the record of God's glorious purposes.'

The man comes over and sits down, presumably oblivious to what is about to take place. Boaz turns to the city fathers, of whom he has gathered a quorum—ten of them. He realises that he is engaged in a legal transaction. He sits them down. None of them has any idea of what is going on. Then Boaz says to the kinsman-redeemer:

> *Naomi, who has come back from the country of Moab, is selling the parcel of land that belonged to our relative Elimelech. So I thought I would tell you of it and say, "Buy it in the presence of those sitting here and in the presence of the elders of my people." If you will redeem it, redeem it.* (4:3-4)[60]

To our surprise— perhaps also to Boaz's and our horror—the anonymous relative replies, 'I will redeem it.'

But Boaz is not finished:

> *The day you buy the field from the hand of Naomi, you also acquire Ruth the Moabite, the widow of the dead, in order to perpetuate the name of the dead in his inheritance.* (4:5)[61]

At this the kinsman-redeemer swallows hard—and now back-pedals:

> *I cannot redeem it for myself, lest I impair my own inheritance. Take my right of redemption yourself . . .* (4:6)

The closer relative

Here is a man who has a covenant responsibility to care for his wider family circle, and to redeem family property in order to maintain it within the family circle. But he is also a shrewd businessman. In the ordinary course of events, redeemed land would default to the original owner in the year of jubilee.[62] In this instance, since Naomi has no sons and no grandsons, it might be thought that would not happen; the redemption price would in effect become a final purchase price. Rather than merely renting and farming the land for a number of years, it would become his and his family's in perpetuity. It sounded like a good deal!

But the new factor—a young widow, still capable of having children—radically changes the value of the investment! He suspected that buying the property might restrict and perhaps burden him financially for a while, but thought it would be a shrewd long-term investment. The short-term hardships and sacrifices would be well worth the potential long-term gain! But he did not bargain for Naomi *and* Ruth! In meeting covenantal obligations and responsibilities, is this man prepared to do so without reservation and potentially at great personal expense? The answer is no.

We are not told whether the relative knew from the start all the implications of purchasing the land, but hoped that they would not be mentioned. But certainly in terms of the narrative, it is clear that Boaz is patiently working his way through the application of the divine Torah to this specific situation, probing his relative's heart all the way. Did he already know this man's reputation for a shrewd financial deal? Did he suspect that he would not be beneath taking as much advantage of Boaz as possible, and 'pulling a fast one' on him?

In his retraction, this anonymous man fits wonderfully into the conclusion of the book. In chapter 1, two young women are faced with a decision—a costly decision of faith. One turns back, and is heard of no more. Now in chapter 4, two men are presented with a costly commitment. One turns back, and his name remains undisclosed for the rest of world history. In this way, the closer relative appears as a kind of foil to Boaz who, by contrast, displays *hesed*—the loyal love that pours itself out in fulfilling covenantal obligations, no matter what the material expense. Therein lies his godliness, his likeness to the great covenant God, who at great expense redeemed his people from Egypt and at infinitely great expense will redeem sinners through the gift of his Son on the cross.

Here, then, is a man who draws lines to limit his liabilities, to limit the obedience that he is prepared to offer within the context of the covenant that God has made with his people. Like the rich young ruler, he has wealth that he must preserve, and so he turns his back on the covenant way; like the priest and the Levite who did body-swerves past the wounded traveller on the Jericho Road, he shows no *hesed*.[63]

But, of course, the relative does not go away before the (to us rather obscure) ceremony of the removal of the shoe has been performed. What lies behind it may be the divine promise given to Joshua: 'Every place that the sole of your foot will tread upon I have given you' (Joshua 1:3). Here it is a graphic expression of a bargain in which land is being transferred. According to the ancient custom, which the author explains (not only to us but even to the original readers of the book of Ruth), the man takes off his sandal, and gives it to Boaz. It appears to have been the rough equivalent of signing the legal deed and shaking hands on the contract. Thus the transaction becomes binding.

The law of the Lord

So much for the narrative of the way in which Boaz becomes the instrument by which the blessing of God is brought to fruition. But this is also an illustration of the life-principle by which all of God's people in every generation are enriched. God's covenant blessing comes to the man or woman who employs the law of the Lord as his or her guide, and the wisdom of the Lord to direct his or her lifestyle.

There would have been people in Bethlehem, who, if they had heard what happened at the threshing floor or what Boaz does in chapter 4, perhaps would have turned their heads in astonishment and said, 'There goes Boaz — what a legalist! What a stickler he is for the law! Why can't he loosen up and enjoy some spiritual freedom?' Yet, clearly, God is teaching us here that his blessings come to us through faithfulness to both the specific directives and the undergirding principles of his covenant commands. Walk in this way and we enter into blessing.

The Old Testament Scriptures abound in examples of this principle. The person who walks in the law of the Lord, meditates on it, makes it his or her delight, is the person who enters into the fullness of God's promised blessings (Psalm 1:1ff.). For such a person there is a health-giving, invigorating effect in obedience. God's wisdom is 'healing to your flesh and refreshment to your bones' (Proverbs 3:8). And there is the bonus of growing in wisdom—even to the point of having more wisdom than the scholars who educate us.[64]

Boaz is a walking illustration of Psalm 119, and of the book of Proverbs. He has hidden the law of the Lord in his heart. It pours out of his life. He has learned to commit his way to the Lord, and to wait in patience for God to act. In this way he learns that the Lord brings his promised blessings to his people in the best way and at the right time. It is important to understand that this is a permanent principle of a covenant lifestyle. If we love the Lord, we will keep his commandments. This, as Jeremiah specifically underlines, is the hallmark of regeneration in the new covenant:

> *Behold, the days are coming, declares the LORD, when I will make a new covenant with the house of Israel and the house of Judah, not like the covenant that I made with their fathers on the day when I took them by the hand to bring them out*

> *of the land of Egypt, my covenant that they broke, though I was their husband, declares the LORD. But this is the covenant that I will make with the house of Israel after those days, declares the LORD: I will put my law within them, and I will write it on their hearts. And I will be their God, and they shall be my people.*[65]

How strange when 'new covenant' believers imagine that the law of God no longer plays a role in the Christian life— since it actually defines that new covenant experience! If it is true that the law of God condemns us and thus drives us to seek Christ because we despair of ourselves, it is also true that Christ by the Spirit enables us to fulfil the law in love in order that, more and more, we may walk in his covenanted ways. Paul underlines this in Romans 8:3-4. In the process of showing how the whole Trinity is involved in our salvation, he also stresses that Christian living involves the fulfilment of God's law:

> *For God has done what the law, weakened by the flesh, could not do. By sending his own Son in the likeness of sinful flesh and for sin, he condemned sin in the flesh, in order that the righteous requirement of the law might be fulfilled in us, who walk not according to the flesh but according to the Spirit.*

The New Testament stresses that, rather than leaving the law behind, the Holy Spirit produces (or reproduces) in us what he has produced here in Boaz—such a love for the Lord that we fulfil his law—and thus the full meaning of God's design comes to expression in our lives.

Older writers used to speak about the grace of law. In our day we, too, need to understand that obedience to the Lord's commands is not legalism, any more than learning the keys on the piano, or following the composer's score, is a form of musical legalism. Rather, it is the means by which we learn to make music! The laws of golf, for example, give all participants in a tournament freedom to play and enjoy the game.[66] How upside-down our world, when a professional sportsman caught cheating, say in a golf tournament, would be publicly shamed and disciplined, but cheating on his wife and breaking the commandments of God might have no impact on his status as icon!

Not so Boaz. He is not presented to us as an icon. He is a hero—true through and through.

So the great transaction takes place; Boaz commits himself publicly to redeeming the land and to marrying Ruth. The wedding takes place, and a child is born. There is blessing upon blessing for the man who walks according to the law of the Lord!

Long before the third chapter of the book of Proverbs was written, and many centuries before the author of Hebrews would cite verses from it as an example of the way God 'addresses you as sons' (Hebrews 12:5), Boaz was a walking, breathing, working model of its wisdom:

> *Let not steadfast love and faithfulness forsake you;*
> *bind them around your neck;*
> *write them on the tablet of your heart.*
> *So you will find favour and good success*
> *in the sight of God and man.*
> *Trust in the Lord with all your heart,*
> *and do not lean on your own understanding.*
> *In all your ways acknowledge him,*
> *and he will make straight your paths.*
> *(Proverbs 3:3-6)*

Blessing from the people and the elders

The departure of both Boaz and Naomi from the stage takes place against the background of two choruses—serving a function similar to that of the chorus in classical Greek drama. In both cases they provide commentary on the events we have witnessed.

The men ask that Boaz and Ruth may be a means of blessing to Israel, as Rachel and Leah were a blessing as mothers of the twelve sons and therefore the twelve tribes. Remarkably, the elders also pray that Boaz's house may be 'like the house of Perez', one of the sons born to Judah through his incest with his daughter-in-law Tamar.

The reference is particularly poignant because the levirate law featured largely in that terrible incident—but without it there would have been no Boaz, as our narrator will make clear a few verses later on! Embedded in Boaz's personal history is an amazing example of how God can weave disaster and sin together into his purposes and produce— a Boaz!

So much for Boaz! What about the Lord's hesed to Ruth? This, too, is marvellous.

Ruth's blessing

From almost the beginning of this book there have been hints of the ultimate blessing Ruth will experience. We saw the first in Naomi's prayer in Ruth 1:8: 'May the LORD deal kindly with you'—may he show *hesed*! Just as Mr Anonymous is a kind of foil over against Boaz and simply disappears from sight, so was Orpah in relation to Ruth. The covenantal blessing of God was as real a possibility for her as for Ruth, but she turned away and we hear no more about her. By contrast, the prayer that Ruth would experience the divine hesed is answered abundantly.

But this is not the only prayer made for Ruth's blessing. Boaz also prayed: 'The LORD repay you . . . the God of Israel, under whose wings you have come to take refuge' (2:12). Ruth finds *hesed* in Boaz's love. The divine reversal begins to take place.

- Ruth left home and family: the Lord gives her a home and a family.
- Ruth made a profoundly costly decision—that she would belong to the Lord and his people, even if nothing else belonged to her, even though one of her most fundamental, God-given, natural instincts to be a wife and mother might never be satisfied.

The possibility that faithfulness to Christ might lead to a life without a husband, without children, is a difficult and challenging issue for many women. The instinct to be a wife and mother might never be satisfied. There can be great personal cost in being faithful to the Lord. It is therefore essential to keep in view that marriage and family are not everything, and that the deepest satisfaction can be found ultimately only in Christ.

But in Ruth the Lord writes in large letters the lessons we need to learn. He is no one's debtor. Ruth's experience foreshadows Paul's words in Ephesians 2:4-7:

> *But God, being rich in mercy, because of the great love with which he loved us, even when we were dead in our trespasses made us alive . . . so that . . . he might show the immeasurable richness of his grace in kindness towards us.*

Many people have hesitated to trust and follow Jesus Christ because they have thought that they could not cope with the potential implications of yielding everything to him. Yet they come to discover that rather than being their debtor, the Lord blesses them in ways far beyond their imagining. That is the kind of God we have. This is what it means to 'take refuge under the wings of El Shaddai'.

This was the language used in Naomi's Bible to describe the God of the Exodus: a mighty eagle swooping down and delivering his children, protecting them under the shadow of his wings, bringing them into the Promised Land.[67] He is our refuge and our strength. He protects us and provides for us. He nourishes us, he guides us, he supplies our need, because he has redeemed us at great personal expense.

This is why there is a simple logic in the teaching of the Bible. If you shelter under the wings of the Almighty, then you can be certain that he will work out everything for your good. It is his declared purpose, sealed at the expense of his Son's death, to bless you. This is the logic of the gospel: if God did not spare his own Son, with his Son he will freely give you all things.[68] It is irrefutable, indestructible logic. It is inconceivable that this generous heavenly Father would suddenly become niggardly.

The heresy of divine niggardliness

Divine niggardliness is no part of biblical teaching, although it sometimes percolates into our thinking. But it is the innuendo of hell, not of heaven. It was employed first by the serpent in the Garden of Eden: Has God set all these trees before your eyes and then said to you, 'You are to eat of none of the trees in this garden?' (see Genesis 3:1). The serpent not only undermined the authority of God's word; *he distorted the character of God himself.*

What God had actually said was: All these trees and their fruit are for you—except one. You can enjoy them all, but I want you to show me that you love and trust me by refusing to eat from one tree (see Genesis 2:16-17).

The serpent exaggerated the limitation, hid the reason for it, and thus distorted and almost destroyed Eve's sense of God's generosity: 'Did God actually say, "You shall not eat of *any tree* in the garden"?' (Genesis 3:1; italics mine).

There is nothing the devil does more subtly (as here with Adam and Eve) than produce in us a confusion of identity, leading us to think about God as though he were malevolent and destructive instead of gracious. In many Christians' lives that distortion lingers on, like a hangover, from our unregenerate past. Disastrously, we become convinced that God has said: 'I am giving you my law, and as a result your life will be constrained and restricted—because I am a niggardly God.' *But that is not the voice of the God of the covenant!* That is not the voice of our Lord Jesus Christ!

No wonder the book of Revelation warns us that there is a demonic creature who looks 'like a lamb, but . . . spoke like a dragon' who 'deceived the inhabitants of the earth' (Rev. 13:11,14 NIV). In contrast, the covenant God of the Bible has opened his heart and given us his Son. He had only one Son and he gave him for us. If that is the case, then we can trust him in and for everything. With Christ God will give us all things.

Naomi

The last of the central characters to leave the stage is Naomi—perhaps an indication that, all along, the story has been about her life. The Lord has now brought his purposes for her full circle. Just as he brought blessing to Boaz and displayed kindness to Ruth, he brings the rich fullness of his *hesed* to empty Naomi. Now she experiences the reversal of the words she spoke on her return: 'Do not call me Naomi . . . the Almighty has dealt very bitterly with me . . . the LORD has brought me back empty' (1:20-21). She was right, of course. The Lord had brought her back empty. But he did so in order to fill her.

At the beginning of the story we saw Naomi holding tightly, as it were, to her husband and grasping the hands of her two boys as together they left Bethlehem. She returned with nothing in her hands: no husband, no children—only the liability of a widowed Moabite daughter-in-law. But as the narrative proceeded, we sensed the possibility that God was, perhaps, going to fill her with his destined fullness.

God does so literally. First he filled Naomi with an abundance of food (chapters 2 and 3). The famine in which she turned from God became the feast she enjoyed when she returned to him. But in this last glimpse of Naomi she is sitting with Boaz's and Naomi's son Obed in her arms. He is a 'handful' for his once empty-handed grandmother! The womenfolk of Bethlehem surround her. They provide commentary on what God has done, like a chorus in a Greek drama, blessing her and praying for her. Her hands are full with a little grandson! And he is the embodiment of the fullness God has given the woman who was 'barren'. Not only has God satisfied her hunger; he has given her a family tree.

God's way

Naomi is one of a series of barren women in Scripture who have offspring, a select group joined together in God's purposes by the way their lives point forward to his final blessing of this barren and empty world. She is preceded by Sarah, mother of Isaac, and by Tamar, mother of Perez; and followed in turn by Hannah, mother of Samuel, and Elizabeth, mother of John the Baptist. These links in the divine chain all point forward to the ultimate miracle prophesied by Isaiah[69]—not just a barren but a virgin woman, who is given a child through the miraculous work of the Holy Spirit—Mary, the mother of our Lord Jesus.

This is God's way. He takes the weak things of this world and through them confounds the things that are mighty; through the things that are low and despised he shames the strong, and through the things that are not he confounds the things that are![70]

Incidentally, the words of verse 15 (which appear to refer to Obed) well express the ministry grandsons may have to their grandmothers! 'He will renew your life and sustain you in your old age' (NIV).

But while Naomi experiences this fullness, we should not be oblivious to the dark night through which she has come. The blessing of the child is real and glorious, but it is not meant to be a substitute for what she has lost. We need to be as realistic as the author of Ruth. Whatever interim blessing and fullness we experience as the community of God's people, there will always be in this world a sense of incompleteness, of 'not-yet-ness'. We lose the most precious possessions in our lives, and in this world nothing can ever take their place. So it is with Naomi.

Is there no final resolution? Yes, there is. But it lies far beyond the lifetime of Naomi.

All's well that ends well

Boaz's *hesed* has led to his marriage to Ruth; her *hesed* has been crowned with his love and their child. Naomi's repentance has brought her God's fullness. At the end of this wonderful story, when Boaz and Ruth have stepped from the stage, Naomi and her grandson are the focus of the attention and the prayers of the women of Jerusalem. 'Blessed be the LORD,' they say, 'who has not left you this day without a redeemer' (4:14).

But notice that they also pray (as the elders had earlier prayed around Boaz) that the fullness of God's purpose in Naomi's life will emerge beyond her own lifetime, in what God will do in and through Obed and others, precisely because of what God has done in and through her—'may his name be renowned in Israel!' (4:14). Surely this must have been the purpose of God in giving her a daughter-in-law who has displayed such *hesed* in her love for her mother-in-law—a daughter-in-law who 'is more to you than seven sons' (v.15, a staggering statement in Jewish—and perhaps any—society!).

Earlier, the elders had prayed that this unlikely marriage would be like the great marriages of former days in the history of God's people, when he had surprised them by weaving together imperfect human activity with his wise sovereignty. But, if anything, these women's prayers are full of even greater insight. They seem to appreciate that the purposes of God through the suffering and loss of Naomi must be greater than can be brought to completion in the span of one lifetime. The abiding significance of God's work must lie well beyond Naomi's life in the lives of others.

That is why the story ends with a family tree.

Family trees can be vital

At first sight the closing verses of Ruth may seem to us to be an anticlimax—if we even bother to read them at all. Why end this beautiful story with a family tree, a piece of dusty historical information about long-dead people? But the final words of the book of Ruth are actually the most important in the book and contain its deepest message. The final sentence sets the previous four chapters in an entirely new light!

This is storytelling at its best, when the punch line is at the end and takes us completely by surprise:

> *Salmon fathered Boaz,*
> *Boaz fathered Obed,*
> *Obed fathered Jesse,*
> *and Jesse fathered David.*
> (*4:21-22*)

This is David's family tree. Yes, *that* David—King David!

Now follow the steps:

- no emigration—no return of Ruth;
- no Ruth—no marriage to Boaz;

- no marriage to Boaz—no Obed;
- no Obed—no Jesse;
- no Jesse—no David.

Obviously, then, the book of Ruth in the form in which we have it in our Bibles was written in the time of David or later. Perhaps its function was to defend the kingship of David and his lineage as legitimate (despite having a Moabitess playing an essential role in it), by demonstrating the hand of God in providence in bringing Ruth to Bethlehem, by clarifying her spiritual character and by stressing the legality of the marriage between Boaz and Ruth. In a sense, the book is not ultimately about Naomi, or Ruth, or Boaz, or even Obed. It is about the great king of Israel!

There is a broad and general lesson to be learned here. The explanation for much that takes place in our lives lies well beyond our own lives, and may be hidden from us all through our lives! For God does not mean to touch only *our* lives by what he does in us; he has the lives of others in view—even those yet unborn.

That is why life can seem so untidy for the people of God. He has not yet finished his business. There may be many loose ends. The tapestry is only partially complete. He has still much weaving to do in which he will bring these loose ends together, perhaps in someone else's life in the future—long after we are gone. God means to bring blessings and answers to prayer beyond anything we could ever ask or imagine—just as he did here. As Hebrews chapter 11 makes clear, it is a mark of genuine faith to look beyond our own day to the time when God will fulfil his promises.

One last step

But even this is not the final explanation of the depth of God's work in Naomi and Ruth. There is one last step to take.

Even if you have never previously read the closing verses of the book of Ruth, you have probably seen them or heard them read. But where?

This family tree reappears in the opening chapter of the New Testament, in Matthew 1:5-6. For this is not only part of the family tree of King David; it is part of the family tree of King David's greater Son, our Lord Jesus Christ! In that sense, no Ruth—no Saviour. Truly God worked everything together, over hundreds of years, for the ultimate good he had in store for those who love him!

The Bread of Life

This, then, is the final explanation for, and the purpose behind, the trauma of Naomi's experience and the costly pilgrimage of Ruth. What God was quarrying out of the suffering of these two women was nothing less than his purpose to bring his Son into the world in Bethlehem. He had in view not only providing literal bread in Bethlehem for a Gentile woman and her Jewish mother-in-law, but the coming of the Bread of Life, broken not only for Israel but in order to provide salvation for men and women in every place.

Did the author of Ruth catch a glimpse of this—for example, in the messianic shadows that seem to be cast over some of David's psalms about the kingdom of God? We do not know. One thing is sure. God had said to his Son that he would give him the nations for his inheritance (Psalm 2:8). That still lay in the future. But the fact that he went to such lengths to bring a Gentile woman into his purposes was already an indication that he would keep his promise.

How fitting that the book of Ruth was traditionally read at the time of the Feast of Pentecost—the feast that New Testament believers would come to associate with the coronation of great

David's greater Son and the fulfillment of the messianic promise of the Father to his royal Son:

> *Ask of me, and I will make the nations your heritage, and the ends of the earth your possession.* (Psalm 2:8)

William Cowper was surely right:

> *Deep in unfathomable mines*
> *Of never-failing skill,*
> *He treasures up his bright designs*
> *And works his sovereign will.*[71]

Years ago, during a visit to the De Beers' diamond mine in Kimberley, South Africa, I was taken down into the bowels of the earth, there to feel the shudder of the ground as miners blasted into the rock for diamonds. When we came up to the surface again—and had been carefully searched!—the manager of the mine said to us, 'You know, every day we blast away 16,000 tons of rock, and we bring up only a couple of handfuls of diamonds. But it's worth it. *It really is worth it for these precious stones.*'

Naomi, Ruth, Boaz—God has quarried deeply in them. What is his purpose? He is mining for diamonds. And by the end of the book, all three know that it has been worth it. They have experienced God's *hesed.* His faithful love has led them, provided for them and filled them. The story that began for Naomi at a time when there was no king in Israel, became a day when there was no bread in Bethlehem, and then a dark night in which there were no children in her family. Now her covenant-keeping, all-sufficient God, Yahweh and El Shaddai, has given her a grandson, and within a few generations will give Israel its greatest king.

He is a faithful God. He does all things well.

Praise to the Lord, who o'er all things so wondrously reigneth;
Shieldeth thee gently from harm, and when fainting sustaineth.
Hast thou not seen
How thy heart's wishes have been
Granted in what he ordaineth?[72]

Appendix
John Newton on the guidance of God[73]

Dear Sir,

It is well for those who are duly sensible of their own weakness and fallibility, and of the difficulties with which they are surrounded in life, that the Lord has promised to guide his people with his eye, and to cause them to hear a word behind them, saying, 'This is the way, walk ye in it', when they are in danger of turning aside either to the right hand or to the left. For this purpose, he has given us the written word to be a lamp to our feet, and encouraged us to pray for the teaching of his Holy Spirit, that we may rightly understand and apply it.

It is, however, too often seen, that many widely deviate from the path of duty, and commit gross and perplexing mistakes, while they profess a sincere desire to know the will of God, and think they have his warrant and authority. This must certainly be owing to misapplication of the rule by which they judge, since the rule itself is infallible, and the promise sure. The Scripture cannot deceive us, if rightly understood; but it may, if perverted, prove the occasion of confirming us in a mistake. The Holy Spirit cannot mislead those who are under his influence; but we may suppose that we are so, when we are not.

It may not be unseasonable to offer a few thoughts upon a subject of great importance to the peace of our minds, and to the honour of our holy profession.

Many have been deceived as to what they ought to do, or in forming a judgment beforehand of events in which they are nearly concerned, by expecting direction in ways which the Lord has not warranted. I shall mention some of the principal of these, for it is not easy to enumerate them all.

Some persons, when two or more things have been in view, and they could not immediately determine which to prefer, have committed their case to the Lord by prayer, and have then proceeded to cast lots: taking it for granted, that, after such a solemn appeal, the turning up of the lot might be safely rested in as an answer from God.

It is true, the Scripture, and indeed right reason, assures us, that the Lord disposes the lot; and there are several cases recorded in the Old Testament, in which lots were used by Divine appointment; but I think neither these, nor the choosing Matthias by lot to the apostleship, are proper precedents for our conduct.

In the division of the lands of Canaan, in the affair of Achan, and in the nomination of Saul to the kingdom, recourse was had to lots by God's express command. The instance of Matthias likewise was singular, such as can never happen again; namely, the choice of an apostle; who would not have been upon a par with the rest, who were chosen immediately by the Lord, unless He had been pleased to interpose in some extraordinary way; and all these were before the canon of Scripture was completed, and before the full descent and communication of the Holy Spirit, who was promised to dwell with the church to the end of time.

Under the New Testament dispensation, we are invited to come boldly to the Throne of Grace, to make our requests known to the Lord, and to cast our cares upon him: but we have neither precept nor promise respecting the use of lots;

and to have recourse to them without his appointment, seems to be tempting him rather than honouring him, and to savour more of presumption than dependence. The effects likewise of this expedient have often been unhappy and hurtful: a sufficient proof how little it is to be trusted to as a guide of our conduct.

Others, when in doubt, have opened the Bible at a venture, and expected to find something to direct them in the first verse they should cast their eye upon. It is no small discredit to this practice, that the heathens, who knew not the Bible, used some of their favourite books in the same way; and grounded their persuasions of what they ought to do, or of what should befall them, according to the passage they happened to open upon.

Among the Romans, the writings of Virgil were frequently consulted upon these occasions; which gave rise to the well-known expression of the *Sortes Virgilianae*. And indeed Virgil is as well adapted to satisfy inquirers in this way as the Bible itself; for if people will be governed by the occurrence of a single text of Scripture, without regarding the context, or duly comparing it with the general tenor of the word of God, and with their own circumstances, they may commit the greatest extravagances, expect the greatest impossibilities, and contradict the plainest dictates of common sense, while they think they have the word of God on their side.

Can the opening upon 2 Samuel 7:3, when Nathan said unto David, 'Do all that is in thine heart, for the Lord is with thee', be sufficient to determine the lawfulness or expediency of actions? Or can a glance of the eye upon our Lord's words to the woman of Canaan, Matthew 15:28, 'Be it unto thee even as thou wilt', amount to a proof, that the present earnest desire of the mind (whatever it may be) shall be surely accomplished? Yet it is certain that matters big with important consequences have been engaged in, and the most sanguine expectations formed, upon no better warrant than dipping (as it is called) upon a text of Scripture.

A sudden strong impression of a text, that seems to have some resemblance to the concern upon the mind, has been accepted by many as an infallible token that they were right, and that things would go just as they would have them: or, on the other hand, if the passage bore a threatening aspect, it has filled them with fears and disquietudes, which they have afterwards found were groundless and unnecessary. These impressions, being more out of their power than the former method, have been more generally regarded and trusted to, but have frequently proved no less delusive.

It is allowed, that such impressions of a precept or a promise as humble, animate, or comfort the soul, by giving it a lively sense of the truth contained in the words, are both profitable and pleasant; and many of the Lord's people have been instructed and supported (especially in a time of trouble) by some seasonable word of grace applied and sealed by his Spirit with power to their hearts. But if impressions or impulses are received as a voice from heaven, directing to such particular actions as could not be proved to be duties without them, a person may be unwarily misled into great evils and gross delusions; and many have been so. There is no doubt but the enemy of our souls, if permitted, can furnish us with Scriptures in abundance in this way, and for these purposes.

Some persons judge of the nature and event of their designs, by the freedom which they find in prayer. They say they commit their ways to God, seek his direction, and are favoured with much enlargement of spirit; and therefore they cannot doubt but what they have in view is acceptable in the Lord's sight. I would not absolutely reject every plea of this kind, yet, without other corroborating evidence, I could not admit it in proof of what it is brought for.

It is not *always* easy to determine when we have spiritual freedom in prayer. Self is deceitful; and when our hearts are much fixed and bent upon a thing, this may put words and earnestness into our mouths. Too often we first secretly determine for ourselves, and then come to ask counsel of God; in such a disposition we are ready to catch at every thing that may seem to favour our darling scheme; and the Lord, for the detection and chastisement of our hypocrisy (for hypocrisy it is, though perhaps hardly perceptible to ourselves), may answer us according to our idols; see Ezekiel 14:3,4.

Besides, the grace of prayer may be in exercise, when the subject-matter of the prayer may be founded upon a mistake, from the intervention of circumstances which we are unacquainted with. Thus, I may have a friend in a distant country; I hope he *is* alive; I pray for him, and it is my duty so to do. The Lord, by his Spirit, assists his people in what is their present duty. If I am enabled to pray with much liberty for my distant friend, it may be a proof that the Spirit of the Lord is pleased to assist my infirmities, but it is no proof that my friend is certainly alive at the time I am praying for him: and if the next time I pray for him I should find my spirit straitened, I am not to conclude that my friend is dead, and therefore the Lord will not assist me in praying for him any longer.

Once more: A remarkable dream has sometimes been thought as decisive as any of the foregoing methods of knowing the will of God. That many wholesome and seasonable admonitions have been received in dreams, I willingly allow; but, though they may be occasionally noticed, to pay a great attention to dreams, especially to be guided by them, to form our sentiments, conduct, or expectations upon them, is superstitious and dangerous. The promises are not made to those who dream, but to those who watch.

Upon the whole, though the Lord may give to some persons, upon some occasions, a hint or encouragement out of the common way; yet expressly to look for and seek his direction in such things as I have mentioned, is unscriptural and ensnaring. I could fill many sheets with a detail of the inconveniences and evils which have followed such a dependence, within the course of my own observation. I have seen some presuming they were doing God service, while acting in contradiction to his express commands. I have known others infatuated to believe a lie, declaring themselves assured, beyond the shadow of a doubt, of things which, after all, never came to pass; and when at length disappointed, Satan has improved the occasion to make them doubt of the plainest and most important truths, and to account their whole former experience a delusion. By these things weak believers have been stumbled, cavils and offences against the Gospel multiplied, and the ways of truth evil spoken of.

But how then may the Lord's guidance be expected? After what has been premised negatively, the question may be answered in a few words. In general, he guides and directs his people, by affording them, in answer to prayer, the light of his Holy Spirit, which enables them to understand and to love the Scriptures. The word of God is not to be used as a lottery; nor is it designed to instruct us by shreds and scraps, which, detached from their proper places, have no determinate import; but it is to furnish us with just principles, right apprehensions, to regulate our judgments and affections, and thereby to influence and direct our conduct.

They who study the Scriptures, in an humble dependence upon Divine teaching, are convinced of their own weakness, are taught to make a true estimate of every thing around them, are gradually formed into a spirit of submission to the will of God, discover the nature and duties of their several situations and relations in life, and the snares and temptations to which they are exposed. The word of God dwells richly in them, is a preservative from error, a light to their feet, and a spring of strength and consolation. By treasuring up the doctrines, precepts, promises, examples, and exhortations of Scripture, in their minds, and daily comparing themselves with the rule by which they walk, they grow into an habitual frame of spiritual wisdom, and acquire a gracious taste, which enables them to judge of right and wrong with a degree of readiness and certainty, as a musical ear judges of sounds. And they are seldom mistaken, because they are influenced by the love of Christ, which rules in their hearts, and a regard to the glory of God; which is the great object they have in view.

In particular cases, the Lord opens and shuts for them, breaks down walls of difficulty which obstruct their path, or hedges up their way with thorns, when they are in danger of going wrong, by the dispensations of his providence. They know that their concernments are in his hands; they are willing to follow whither and when he leads; but are afraid of going before him. Therefore they are not impatient: because they believe, they will not make haste, but wait daily upon him in prayer; especially when they find their hearts most engaged in any purpose or pursuit, they are most jealous of being deceived by appearances, and dare not move farther or faster than they can perceive his light shining upon their paths. I express at least their desire, if not their attainment: thus they would be. And though there are seasons when faith languishes, and self too much prevails, this is their general disposition; and the Lord, whom they serve, does not disappoint their expectations. He leads them by a right way, preserves them from a thousand snares, and satisfies them that he is and will be their guide even unto death.

I am, & c.

John Newton

Notes

1. The Septuagint was a translation of the Hebrew Bible into Greek, the common language of the world of the New Testament.
2. From the hymn entitled 'Light shining out of Darkness', better known by its first line, 'God moves in a mysterious way', in William Cowper (1731–1800) and John Newton (1725–1807), Olney Hymns, Book III, Hymn 15.
3. Julius Caesar, De Bello Gallico, 1.i.
4. Many Old Testament scholars have come to recognise the extent to which this pattern, so familiar to students of English poetry (A,B,C,D–D,C,B,A), is commonplace in the Bible. It is the story of fall and restoration, death and glory, sin and grace, demolition and reconstruction. Just as the coming of Christ marks the turning point of the whole Bible story, so that story is punctuated by a series of miniature turning points.
5. Just as some rabbis held that when in chapter 3 Boaz awakens in the middle of the night, it is not because of what Ruth has done but because he is getting up to study Torah!
6. While not specifically stated, it is probably to be assumed that marriage with a non-believing Moabite is in view.
7. The Confession of Faith (1647), XV, 1-2. Italics mine.
8. From the hymn of Charles Wesley (1707-88), 'O Jesus, full of pardoning grace'.
9. The expression is that of the prophet Ezekiel (Ezek. 14:3,4,7).
10. Mark 10:17-31; Romans 7:7-12.
11. John Newton, 'Glorious things of thee are spoken' in Olney Hymns, Book I, Hymn 60.

12. William Cowper, 'God moves in a mysterious way'.
13. Significantly it is the covenant name of God that Naomi uses.
14. William Cowper, 'God moves in a mysterious way'.
15. As Mary, the mother of Jesus, would also later understand (cf. Luke 1:46-55).
16. It is difficult to be certain whether the words 'whose kindness' refer to Boaz or to the Lord. In effect, the two are so integrally related that it makes little difference to the narrative.
17. See Hebrews 10:26-31.
18. See Deuteronomy 28:58-68.
19. Ruth 'clung' to Naomi (1:14) and told her not to urge her to 'leave' her (1:16). These two verbs are used in Genesis 2:24 of Adam and Eve and of marriage ('a man shall leave his father and his mother and hold fast to his wife'). The combination is unusual, and must have been heard as a clear echo of the well-known words in Genesis 2. Perhaps the author is already evoking the atmosphere of marriage, for this language was fundamentally appropriate to the relationship of a man and woman, not a woman and her mother-in-law. At the same time, the vocabulary hints at the remarkable character of Ruth's devotion to Naomi. Like the hesed of marriage love, her love for Naomi is rooted in her hesed towards the Lord, which in turn is rooted in his hesed towards her!
20. Cf. Genesis 2:18.
21. Cf. Genesis 2:21-23.
22. The verb 'to rejoice' (kauchoōmai) in Romans 5:2,3,11 has the same root as the noun 'boasting' (kauchēsis) in Romans 3:27.
23. Here such biblical teaching as Genesis 12:1-2, Psalm 2:8, Isaiah 52:13-15 lies behind the wording of the 'Grear Commission'.

24. See J. Meeter, Selected Shorter Writings of Benjamin B. Warfield, vol. 1 (Presbyterian & Reformed, Phillipsburg, 1970), pp.383-4.
25. Cf. Titus 2:7-10.
26. J. Meeter, p.384.
27. Cf. Matthew 25:31-46.
28. The word translated 'reproach' in 2:15 is used in Genesis 20:6 with sexual overtones.
29. John Milton, The Second Defence of the People of England Against an Anonymous Libel, translated from the Latin by Robert Fellowes. Downloaded from: http://www.constitution.org/milton/second_defence.htm.
30. 1 Corinthians 2:14-15.
31. The word translated 'cloak' (3:3) is used in the Song of Solomon for the fragrant robes of the beloved.
32. See the ritual of taking off the shoe (4:7), which the author later explains.
33. Note the beautiful expression of this in Psalm 103:4, where God's redemptive work is seen as the incentive for covenant praise of him: 'Bless the LORD . . . who redeems your life from the pit.' The title 'Redeemer' is, of course, a wonderfully appropriate one for the Lord Jesus Christ.
34. It is assumed already in Geness 38:8-10 and taught in Deuteronomy 25:5-10.
35. Cf. the same expression in the context of the divine marriage with Israel in the poignantly expressive description of God's covenant with her in Ezekiel 16:8.
36. Cf. Hosea 9:1.
37. The Works of John Newton (1820; reprinted Banner of Truth Trust, Edinburgh, 1985), vol. 1, p.331. The letter in which Newton employs this metaphor is one of the finest short statements on the Lord's guidance anywhere to be found and is reprinted as an appendix on pp.149-57. It is also reprinted with other wise counsel from Newton in the fine

selection, Letters of John Newton (Banner of Truth Trust, London, 1958), pp.77-82.

38. Thomas Watson, A Body of Divinity (1692; republished Banner of Truth Trust, London, 1958), p.123.
39. The great seventeenth-century Puritan John Owen took a certain delight in his day in dressing in a manner that gave the lie to the caricature of 'Puritans' in which those who despised their evangelical faith seemed to delight both then and now—apparently Spanish leather boots were his footwear of choice!
40. Boaz's counsel in 3:13-14 makes it clear that the moral reputations of both Boaz and Ruth are in danger.
41. Acts 27:13-44.
42. Mark 4:35-41.
43. Acts 12:6-19.
44. Philippians 4:7.
45. Cited by Sereno E. Dwight, 'Memoir of Jonathan Edwards', Works of Jonathan Edwards (1834), 1, p.xx.
46. See Luke 22:31-32, where Jesus prays for Peter, and John 17:6-11, where he prays for the disciples he protected.
47. This statement seems to confirm the common notion that there was some age-gap between Boaz and Ruth. That said, the seriousness and commitment of a man like Boaz may make him appear much older than his contemporaries.
48. The Journals of Kierkegaard, 1834–1854, edited and translated by Alexander Dru (Collins, London, 1958), p.190. Italics mine.
49. Notice the citation of Isaiah 42:3 with specific reference to Jesus in Matthew 12:20.
50. 1 Kings 7:21; 2 Chronicles 3:17.
51. The words of the exalted Lord Jesus to the angel of the church in Philadelphia are intriguing in this context: 'The one who conquers, I will make him a pillar in the temple of my God' (Revelation 3:12).

52. Particularly in Ephesians 5:22-33.
53. From the hymn of Martin Luther (1483–1546), 'A mighty fortress is our God', translated by F. H. Hedge.
54. Note especially the teaching of Hebrews 2:11-18.
55. Cf. Jeremiah 18:1-6.
56. Constance E. Padwick, Temple Gairdner of Cairo (SPCK, London, 1929), p.92.
57. Ibid., p.57.
58. Hamlet, Act V, scene ii, line 10.
59. From the hymn by Samuel John Stone (1839–1900), 'The Church's one foundation'.
60. It goes without saying that as a good storyteller the narrator of Ruth does not burden us with explanations of all the details—some of them possibly complex—of the laws and customs behind the unfolding of the plot, though he does explain the shoe tradition later described in verse 7. He seems to assume that his readers are familiar with the obligations that went along with the redemption of the land. Much scholarly literature on Ruth has discussed whether in fact levirate law was operative here, since neither Boaz nor the anonymous kinsman was Mahlon's brother (interestingly, it is only at 4:10 that we learn which of the brothers Ruth had married). We have already suggested that in keeping with the way our Lord interpreted the law of God (Matthew 5:17-48), living in God's law (Torah—instruction) involved fulfilling not only its letter but its principles. It is also possible, even likely, that given the structure of the extended family, 'brother' may refer to close male relations and not simply to those born of the same set of parents. Certainly the grace-spirit was to be applied in the life of the covenant community. Happily, while such detailed understanding may be important to the scholar's profession, and informative for us all, it is not essential to our appreciation of the plot.

61. In terms of the law code of the Old Testament it is not altogether clear how the field belonged to Naomi. Inheritance was always on the male side of a family. She may have had rights in it following the death of her husband and sons. In any event, Proverbs 15:25 suggests that the heart of God should determine the application of the law of the land: 'The LORD tears down the house of the proud, but maintains the widow's boundaries.'
62. See Leviticus 25:23ff.
63. Luke 10:25-37.
64. Psalm 119:99.
65. Jeremiah 31:31-33, cited in Hebrews 8:8-12 and 10:15-18.
66. Evangelical Christians often regard any ongoing importance of the law in the Christian life as 'legalism'. In this context it is interesting to notice that every two years or so the governing body of golf, The Royal and Ancient Golf Club of St Andrews, publishes a 500-plus page volume detailing decisions about how the laws of golf apply in situations that have perplexed golfers during that period. Yet no honest golfer regards following the rules as being 'legalistic'! The rules are essential to the game, and to the enjoyment of it. The Christian no less thinks of God's law—the ten principles applicable in every life situation—as 'the law of liberty' (James 1:25).
67. See Exodus 19:4 and Deuteronomy 32:11.
68. See Romans 8:32.
69. See Isaiah 7:14; Matthew 1:18-25.
70. See 1 Corinthians 1:27-28.
71. From the hymn of William Cowper, 'God moves in a mysterious way'.
72. From the hymn by Joachim Neander (1650–80), 'Praise to the Lord, the Almighty', translated by Catherine Winkworth (1828–78) and others.
73. A letter written by John Newton to a correspondent anxious

to have advice about receiving God's guidance and knowing his will. From The Works of John Newton (1820; reprinted by the Banner of Truth Trust, Edinburgh, 1985), vol. 1, pp.324-31. The letter is also reprinted in The Letters of John Newton (Banner of Truth Trust, London, 1960). It is a rare example of spiritual wisdom and practical and pastorally sensitive biblical teaching.